The Baptist and Christian Character of Baylor

The Baptist
and
Christian Character
of
Baylor

Edited by

Donald D. Schmeltekopf

and

Dianna M. Vitanza

with

Bradley J. B. Toben

Baylor University
Waco, TX 76798

Library of Congress Cataloging-in-Publication Data

The Baptist and Christian character of Baylor / edited by Donald D.
Schmeltekopf and Dianna Vitanza ; with Bradley J.B. Toben.
        p. cm.
Includes bibliographical references.
    ISBN 0-914108-05-0
    1. Baylor University—Congresses. 2. Baptist universities and
colleges—Texas—Congresses. I. Schmeltekopf, Donald D.
II. Vitanza, Dianna. III. Toben, Bradley J. B.

    LD353.B37 2003
    378.764'284—dc22

                                                2003023503

Printed in the United States of America on acid-free paper

Special thanks to Becky Parker of The Cowley Group for design
consultation and to Gayle D. Smith of Joe Christensen, Inc. for
printing consultation.

Contents

Part Three
What Does it Mean to Support the
"Mission" of a Christian University?

Conclusion

Editors' Note

The book before you is the culmination of an initiative undertaken by the Council of Deans of Baylor University. Under the leadership of Bradley J. B. Toben, Dean of the Law School at Baylor, the Council of Deans sponsored a two-day, university-wide colloquy on April 10-11, 2003, entitled "The Baptist and Christian Character of Baylor." All the speakers and respondents for the colloquy were assured that the colloquy was to be of such quality that every paper would merit publication in a volume to be published after the conference. Since the two of us have worked together for many years at Baylor and have collaborated on numerous writing projects, we were asked to serve as co-editors, even though one of us might appear to have had a greater personal interest in the project. We believe that our objectivity and integrity as co-editors have not been compromised by the fact that the Council of Deans' purpose in planning the colloquy was to honor one of us, Donald Schmeltekopf, retiring Provost and Vice President for Academic Affairs of Baylor.

The idea for the colloquy and this publication emerged from a meeting of the Council of Deans in November 2002. In an unusual departure from the standard agenda of this group, the Council of Deans agreed to devote its entire November meeting to a discussion of a series of papers from the University of Notre Dame under the general theme "Conversation on the Catholic Character of Notre Dame" presented in 1994. The debate then going on at Notre Dame regarding its religious identity seemed particularly relevant to some of the burning questions and issues occupying our minds at Baylor. As our discussion came to a close, it was clear to all present—ten deans, the chair of the Faculty Senate, and the Provost—that a conference of the kind held at Notre Dame would be useful, stimulating, and timely for Baylor. The title for the conference was right before our collective eyes, "A Colloquy on the Baptist and Christian Character of Baylor." The deans agreed soon thereafter that the Council of Deans would sponsor the event, under the leadership of the Law School.

We believe this colloquy was important for many reasons, but we would like to specify three. First, it provided an opportunity for Baylor faculty members, administrators, and others in attendance to think in a fairly systematic way about the nature of our deepest religious convictions and about how these convictions might contribute to our excellence as a Christian university. Second, the intellectual weight of the colloquy was provided overwhelmingly by Baylor faculty members who represent diverse perspectives on the issues. Third, the conference was an open and free debate—an argument in the best sense of the word—on the most fundamental issues facing Baylor today, especially those surrounding the academic mission and aspirations of the university.

We hope you the reader find this collection of essays enlightening and thought provoking, whether you are identified with Baylor, with another church-related college or university, or with the wider American higher education community. We wish to thank all who contributed to this volume, but especially we wish to thank the Council of Deans for sponsoring what we believe was one of the truly important events in the recent intellectual life of Baylor, and, perhaps, in the world of Christian higher education today.

The editors would like to note their indebtedness to the following members of the *Baylor Law Review* who assisted in the editing and authority cite checking of this manuscript: Geoff Culbertson (the editor-in-chief of the *Law Review*), Jonathan Brush, Carrie Carter, Joseph Price, Scott Snellings, J.R. Vicha, and Susan Whatley. We also wish to thank Becky Shulda, Jami Symank, and Linda Lampert for their help with manuscript preparation.

We are pleased to dedicate this book to the faculty members of Baylor University—past and present. The greatness that is Baylor's is owing primarily and overwhelmingly to the work of her faculty over the years. We are proud to be among its number.

Donald D. Schmeltekopf
Provost Emeritus and the Hazel and Harry Chavanne Professor of Christian Ethics in Business

Dianna M. Vitanza
Associate Professor of English

November 2003
Waco, Texas

Foreword

Bradley J. B. Toben

The title of this book is accurate, but like most titles, it is not especially revealing. Most would pick up this book and nod in simple assent, "Why yes, Baylor University is Baptist and, yes, it does regard itself as a Christian university. So what?"

The title *The Baptist and Christian Character of Baylor* gives only a small clue about the vigorous, pitched debate and conversation, of both an intellectual and practical character, that animate this work. The pages that follow bear witness to a plan and a resulting controversy that have gripped the Baylor community in recent years. The papers of this collection, arising from a colloquy encounter in the Spring of 2003, describe, analyze, and critique a vision embodied in a plan that proposes an aggressive transformation of Baylor.

The much-lauded architect Daniel H. Burnham admonished us all to "dream no small dream, because it hath not the power to move men's souls." Be assured that the plan—described by many as brilliant and invigorating and by others as misguided and corrosive—has moved in some fashion the soul of virtually every man and woman within the Baylor community. It touches upon nearly every aspect of the university in all of its embodiments, functions, and objectives. The plan, called "Baylor 2012," gazes out over a span of about a dozen years—from the point of the plan's development and conceptualization in 2000 and 2001, to its anticipated culmination in 2012—and envisions a Baylor of a higher and sharper profile.

The conversation and the controversy have unfolded against a backdrop that must necessarily inform any meaningful understanding of Baylor. Thus, some background is in order. The university was chartered in 1845 and has for over a century and a half been guided by its mission to provide Christian higher education. The mission statement proclaims that

Baylor is founded on the belief that God's nature is made known through both revealed and discovered truth. Thus, the University derives its understanding of God, humanity, and nature from many sources: the person and work of Jesus Christ, the biblical record, and Christian history and tradition, as well as scholarly and artistic endeavors.

The statement then continues, "[w]ithout imposing religious conformity, Baylor expects the members of its community to support its mission."

Over the years Baylor's faith affiliation and, implicitly, its mission have often been at the center of controversy and debate. In 1990, amid such strife, the charter of the university was amended to make the governing board (now called the Board of Regents) predominantly self-perpetuating. The purpose of the change, bravely conceived and executed by former President Herbert H. Reynolds, was to assure that the governing board of Baylor would never be overtaken by the wave of fundamentalism that had been sweeping, since the late 1970s, through the Southern Baptist Convention and presumptively would eventually sweep beyond the SBC itself and into the state Baptist conventions. The university had reservations about the future character of the Baptist General Convention of Texas, which controlled Baylor's governing board. The ensuing troubled times in the relationship between Baylor and the BGCT could be fairly described as one that might arise if someone turned to a spouse and said, "I love you now, but I also fear the person you may become some day, so I'm going to distance myself in our relationship right now."

Time, perspective, and joint endeavor over the passing years have healed the earlier troubled waters of Baylor in its relationship with the BGCT, which continues to be solidly "moderate" in character. Robert B. Sloan, Jr., succeeded Dr. Reynolds as president in 1995, and in 2000, building upon prior discussions and reflections in the university community regarding the future path of Baylor, President Sloan began actively to develop the plan that eventually came to be known as Baylor 2012.

A deep divide of opinion and sentiment congealed quickly around Baylor 2012. The ensuing discussion has found its content in good-faith expressions of deeply held conviction as well as in sometimes biting statements, both public and private, either supporting or taking aim at the vision. The discussion or—for an institution that prides itself on being the "Baylor family"—perhaps more appropriately, the argument continues to unfold in all manner of venues.

The media has carried the story of the struggle for the heart and soul of Baylor nearly *ad nauseam*, covering a whole range of issues including not only those touching upon faith matters in the context of higher education, but also upon other matters of import, including academic rankings, university financing methods, tuition affordability, the issue of the relative importance of teaching and research, and the often related issue of the relative importance of undergraduate versus graduate education. The nature of the university's organized relationship with its alumni, the impact of changes upon the university's relationships with its traditional constituencies, and disaffection over components of the athletic program and other matters also have received extensive media coverage.

Many who will read these proceedings will be familiar, at least generally, with the matters that occurred both before and after the colloquy and that are ongoing as this collection of papers is being published. In the fall of 2003, a Faculty Senate vote of no-confidence in Dr. Sloan's leadership passed 26-6, although there were many cogent and strongly put assertions, public and private, that the Senate vote did not reflect the sentiments of the larger university faculty. Days later, the Board of Regents spoke loudly in support of President Sloan and Baylor 2012 in a 31-4 reaffirmation of confidence in his leadership and the university's direction.

So it has been that the summer and fall seasons of 2003 have seen the convergence of the turmoil on and beyond the campus of Baylor as its direction and character have been sharply debated. Sadly, too, in the midst of the struggle for the future of Baylor, the men's basketball program experienced both tragedy and scandal.

I work within a discipline—the law—which holds as an article of faith that the truth of any matter is best discerned through the head-to-head competition of ideas elucidated by evidence and argumentation. The art of advocacy, in the legal arena or otherwise, turns upon a basic trust in the notion that ideas, positions, and contentions must be vigorously "put to the test." This testing is best carried out in the direct clash of advocates wielding their best powers of exposition, synthesis, thematic logic, persuasion, demeanor, and argumentation, all set against a framework of the adduced evidence, both tangible and intangible.

This testing by advocacy is embodied in the classic concept of what has come to be known as the "marketplace of ideas," articulated by Justice Oliver Wendell Holmes in his much celebrated dissent in *Abrams v. United States*, 250 U.S. 616 (1919):

> But when men have realized that time has upset many fighting faiths, they may come to believe even more than they believe the very foundations of their own conduct that the ultimate good desired is better reached by free trade in ideas—that the best test of truth is the power of the thought to get itself accepted in the competition of the market, and that truth is the only ground upon which their wishes safely can be carried out.

This powerful observation of Justice Holmes is the essential philosophical justification of the right to free speech in our United States Constitution.

After some time of unrest on the Baylor campus regarding Baylor 2012 and the direction of the university in its faith mission, it appeared evident that it was time to provide a venue for an open, collective conversation about the character and future of the university—and especially about the issues raised within the context of Baylor 2012 concerning faculty hiring, promotion, tenure, and service. We needed to raise the discussions and debates out of the limited, albeit valuable, venues of private discussion and argumentation in offices, on e-mails, in the hallways, and the like. We, therefore, conceived of a university-wide forum for the airing of thoughts— misgivings, enthusiasm, opposition, and even wonderment about our school's direction. So the Law School and the Council of Deans undertook to provide such a forum for the airing of the disparate views on Baylor 2012 and the integrally related issue of the implementation of the faith mission of the university. On April 10-11, 2003, a well-received colloquy took place at the Walter and Sheila Umphrey Law Center, the home of Baylor Law School on the Baylor University campus.

The papers included in this volume were authored, with one exception, by Baylor colleagues who took part, by invitation, in the colloquy as presenters and as respondents. When inviting the various participants to address the colloquy, we sought to bring together a variety of views on the issues before us, and thus we developed a roster of participants known first and foremost for their distinctive insights and perspectives.

Some presenters and respondents at the colloquy have had decades of experience at Baylor under as many as three presidential administrations, while others joined the Baylor faculty within the last few years, in many cases attracted, at least in part, by the promise of Baylor 2012. Some came from the humanities, some from the social sciences, some from the natural sciences, and some from the professions. Some have been ardent advocates of Baylor 2012. Some have regarded it as an unfortunate departure from traditional undergraduate-focused, financial, and operational protocols at Baylor, and as an overbearing attempt to cast Baylor in the mold, not just of a university in a Christian setting and environment, but rather of an aggressively evangelical institution demanding conformity that would stifle true and unfettered intellectual expression and free inquiry.

The papers in this volume make clear that at least in regard to the matters that most directly affect the Baylor faculty, the swirling assertions and counter-assertions that have filled the air at Baylor appear not so much to concern the mission itself but rather, in a manner of point/counterpoint discourse, to revolve principally around the way the mission is to be implemented. Thus, the issues that have been debated with the most fervency focus on questions concerning what role the mission should play in matters of faculty hiring, in the requirements bearing upon promotion and tenure, and in the concept of service. How does the university's faith mission interface with classroom teaching? With research agendas? With service within the university and the community? With a faculty member's involvement in a church or faith community?

These are issues upon which there are markedly differing perspectives, formed by widely differing life experiences, faith traditions, discipline cultures, and, more particularly, by contrasting notions of what Baylor should be "all about." Indeed, in the past some have seen Baylor primarily as a university with "a very fine undergraduate program—a program that is focused on teaching and the development of mentor relationships, and [as it is often remarked] a really good law school."

Those who hold this traditional view of Baylor ask what, if anything, must be sacrificed in our traditional area of prominence in the undergraduate arena, especially in the craft of teaching, to pursue an admittedly ambitious goal in graduate education, along with heightened scholarly expectations across the faculty. Others ask whether the vision should be seen even more broadly as a faith mandate to broaden the university's sphere of inquiry and influence to encompass a significantly supported and ambitious graduate and scholarly agenda. This faith mandate would intertwine the traditional emphases of the university with an energized and renewed effort to address the inter-connectivity of the disciplines, and more importantly, the whole and boundless sphere of God, humankind, and nature.

It was appropriate that the colloquy that explored these important issues also marked the completion of twelve years of service by Donald Schmeltekopf as Provost of Baylor University. I was appointed as dean of the Law School in 1991, a year after Don's arrival and just after he assumed the position of provost. My tenure as dean of the Law School—roughly spanning Don's tenure as provost and spanning parts of the administrations of two presidents—has allowed me to observe first-hand the remarkable academic progress that the university has made under Don's leadership at the academic helm.

Accordingly, a few personal words are in order about this remarkable gentleman and accomplished academician and administrator. Don's many years of service have been marked by notable and far-reaching advances in the academic ends of the university. The significant improvement of our reputation in the circles of higher education and the enhancement of the quality of what we bring to our students in their educational experience over the last many years have not occurred by happenstance. Rather, the changes have come about because, as my own Law School colleagues know that I am fond of saying, "someone is waking up worrying about it and someone is going to bed worrying about it." Don has been that person for our university—the guardian of our best academic traditions and the catalyst for the expansion and refinement of our academic influence in concert with the stated mission of the university.

Don has also brought definition to the position of provost as the point of academic leadership and academic program administration within the university. He has over the past many years—both organizationally and functionally—created a new culture of coordination and camaraderie among the deans of the ten schools of the university. Don introduced and cultivated practices of goal setting, planning, and evaluation within each of the academic units—a most formidable, and very critical, component in the future success of Baylor. He has been, in regard to each of our academic programs, both a strong advocate and, when appropriate, a constructive critic.

He has done all of this with grace, direction, and finesse, all within the context of collegiality and friendship.

I also have had the blessing of a personal friendship with Don. The Law School has made very demonstrable, significant strides over the last several years because we have such a committed team both inside and outside the school. I have been blessed to have leaders – President Robert Sloan; Don; his successor, David Lyle Jeffrey; the university's chief financial officer, David Brooks, and his predecessor, Harold Cunningham, who have understood the unique and distinctive aspects of the culture and success of the Law School. For this reason, it was a special personal and professional pleasure for the Law School, in conjunction with the Council of Deans, to be the principal sponsor of the colloquy that celebrated Don's impact upon the Baylor we all love.

Also fitting is an important note about Judy Schmeltekopf, Don's committed life partner and help-mate. All that I have noted about Don and his successes as our academic leader are indirectly applicable as well to Judy. We all know that with any truly successful husband and wife team, the spouses' respective personal successes would not be possible without the energy and focus that each spouse brings to a long, happy, and healthy marriage. Somehow, I think of this volume as just one testament to the lives of Don and Judy lived truly and well.

Don then leaves a legacy of marked achievement. He has not only led Baylor in its academic mission to great accomplishments and enhanced profile, but most importantly, he has insisted upon excellence in each of our academic endeavors in the classroom, the lab, the studio, and each other venue. He has also been a key player in conceptualizing a future for Baylor that calls for an admittedly aggressive reach for an excellence unparalleled in our past. This quest would explore the animation of every discipline, as appropriate, by the Maker in whom we profess our faith and reliance.

A closing anecdote is in order here. Don is a very competitive guy. In each of his twelve years as provost, he held a two-day deans' retreat in mid-August. And remember . . . we're in Texas. At the end of the first afternoon, Don perennially insisted upon a volleyball match, always consisting of two full games with only a few minutes' break. The court was always laid out on a hillside of parched Texas turf, so one team had to play uphill, looking into the dazzling sun (fortunately, teams rotated sides between games). I've witnessed all twenty-four games these past twelve years. Hard as it may be to believe, Don always—yes, always—was on the winning team.

He fights every point and contests (sometimes with aplomb . . . and sometimes without) every close call. He just hates to lose . . . and he doesn't. Somehow, there's a lesson here. Academic leadership is an amalgam of vision, articulation, persuasion, tactfulness, sensitivity, diplomacy, sincerity, sacrifice, self-deprecation, and persistence. Every leader who leaves a legacy of achievement must bring these attributes to bear in his or her own personal alchemy of leadership. Don has brought to bear his own inimitable style to his leadership as provost. It has been, and continues to be, my privilege to be his friend and to enjoy the fruits of his legacy. In volleyball and otherwise—I have been blessed to be on his team!

Contributors

Robert M. Baird, Professor and Chair of Philosophy and Master Teacher

James Bennighof, Professor of Music Theory, Director of Academic Studies, and Vice Provost for Academic Affairs

Marianna A. Busch, Professor and Chair of Chemistry and Biochemistry

Gerald B. Cleaver, Assistant Professor of Physics

Marjorie J. Cooper, Professor of Marketing

C. Stephen Evans, University Professor of Philosophy and Humanities

Diana R. Garland, Professor and Chair of Social Work and Director, Center for Family and Community Ministries

Owen Lind, Professor of Biology

Byron P. Newberry, Associate Professor of Engineering and Immediate Past Chair, University Tenure Committee

Roger E. Olson, Professor of Theology

Mark Osler, Assistant Professor of Law

Mikeal C. Parsons, Professor and Macon Chair in Religion

M. David Rudd, Professor of Psychology and Neuroscience and Director, Psy.D. Program

Donald D. Schmeltekopf, Provost Emeritus and The Hazel and Harry Chavanne Professor of Christian Ethics in Business

David Solomon, H. B. and W. P. White Director of the Center for Ethics and Culture, University of Notre Dame and former Visiting Distinguished Professor at Baylor

Bradley J. B. Toben, Dean, Law School

Dianna M. Vitanza, Associate Professor of English

Charles A. Weaver, III, Professor of Psychology and Neuroscience and Immediate Past Chair, Faculty Senate

Ralph C. Wood, University Professor of Theology and Literature

Chapter 1

Introduction

A Christian University in the Baptist Tradition: History of a Vision

Donald D. Schmeltekopf

I

In 1852, seven years after the founding of Baylor University in 1845, John Henry Newman gave a series of lectures in Dublin, Ireland, on the nature of a university—in particular, on the nature of a Catholic university. These lectures were later published as *The Idea of a University*, and the book remains one of the most important works on higher education in the English-speaking world. There is no direct relationship between the founding of the Catholic university in Dublin, which prompted Newman's lectures, and the founding of Baylor University. However, it is an interesting and significant historical fact that when the Roman Catholics decided that a university should be established in Ireland, the archbishop invited this distinguished theologian and priest to address the Catholic laypeople of Ireland to stimulate their thinking theologically about what a Catholic university ought to be and to persuade them that such an institution was necessary for educating Catholic youth in their country. On the other hand, when the Baptists of the Republic of Texas decided to found a Baptist university on the Texas frontier, they did not turn to theologians or philosophers to reflect on what such a university might be, but they rather turned to ministers and lawyers and other laypeople who had the practical know-how to establish such an institution and then simply just did it.

For most of Baylor's history, beginning with the opening of classes in Independence, Texas, the university has followed this pragmatic approach to maintaining its Baptist and Christian character. This is not to say that Baylor had no founding vision. In 1844 the Texas Baptist Education Society, created in 1841 for the purpose of promoting religious educational interests, passed the following resolution: "Resolved to found a Baptist university in Texas upon a plan so broad that the requirements of existing conditions would be fully met, and that would be susceptible of enlargement and development to meet the needs of all the ages to come."[1] Within a year Baylor University was chartered and several Texas communities began bidding for it to be placed in their locale. Nothing was said, however, about what makes a university, let alone what makes a Baptist university. It was simply understood by all the founders that religious educational pursuits were important for the training of ministers as well as of those who sought secular learning. After all, this had been the view of Baptists—and many other Protestants. Baptist schools in Rhode Island (Brown University) and Georgia (Mercer Institute) had already provided concrete examples of Baptist higher education to some of Baylor's founding leaders.[2]

This common-sense perspective on the Baptist and Christian character of Baylor was evident in its curriculum from the very beginning. Instruction in and study of the Bible occurred largely on Sundays in the local churches around Independence. There was no requirement for courses in theology, except for students pursuing ministerial training. On the other hand, the required curriculum was made up of courses in Greek, Latin, literature, and history, as well as in science and mathematics. For example, in 1873 the courses of study in the "male college" at Baylor were English, Latin, Greek, mathematics, natural science, French, Spanish, German, Hebrew, ethics, and metaphysics. This sort of curriculum reflected common practice in colleges and universities at the time. Whereas Newman saw all knowledge as divided into three distinct but related parts— God, nature, and human beings ("man")—Baylor's curriculum in its first two decades was divided into three practical "departments"—the preparatory department, the male department, and the female department. These departments were both social and educational in nature. Newman's idea of the connectedness of all knowledge into a coherent whole was of minimal concern to the Baylor of Independence.

Further evidences of a pragmatic approach to the religious identity of Baylor were the campus ethos and the behavioral expectations required of everyone. In 1886, as the move to Waco, Texas, was about to be consummated, Rufus Burleson, former president at Independence and then president-elect for the new campus in Waco, made this statement to a group of students: "Baylor University, for at least a thousand years to come, may be the nursery not merely of great scholars and orators, but of noble women, patriotic citizens, and devoted Christians." He also prayed that "nothing vile or profane may ever enter here, but that these beautiful grounds and magnificent buildings to be erected may be consecrated wholly to innocent joys, to learning, to purity, to patriotism, and to piety."[3]

At that time in Baylor's history, chapel attendance was required of all students every weekday, as were Sabbath school and worship services on Sundays. A vast number of rules and regulations regarding student conduct on campus were in place, enforced by a rigid system of demerits. These various rules and expectations were not unique to Baylor, of course, but at Baylor they were more than rules. They reflected a vital part of the religious character of the university. As the *Baylor Catalogue* of 1856 states,

> One great object of the Faculty will ever be to imbue the minds and hearts of young men with a high sense of honor, integrity and moral excellence. While nothing of a denominational character is taught, very special attention is paid to the Bible recitation and to the Sabbath School instruction; and every student is required to attend public worship at such place as his parent or guardian may designate.[4]

The university's founders needed no new book on the subject of student conduct in order to embrace these standards.

While all the principal founders of Baylor—R. E. B. Baylor, William M. Tryon, and James Huckins—were Baptists, as were most of the original trustees, the institution's first faculty member, Henry F. Gillette, was an active Episcopalian who had migrated from Connecticut a few years earlier. However, there is little information about the religious affiliation of Baylor faculty members recorded for the next fifty years or so. Indeed, such records are not available until

1957-1958, in a report of the Baptist General Convention of Texas, which indicates that 64 percent of Baylor's faculty was Baptist.[5] In 1978 the Board of Trustees mandated that at least half of the faculty should be Baptist. This policy was adopted from the Report of the Long-Range Plans Review Committee. In the section under "Academic Affairs," the report includes this paragraph:

> Faculty members employed by Baylor should possess a clear-cut religious commitment with at least half of the faculty being members of the Southern Baptist denomination. Southern Baptists will continue to be given preference in employment, with evangelical Christian and Protestant groups next, followed by other Christians and Jews. Prospective faculty members will be explicitly informed at the time of initial interview that Baylor is a church-related institution that takes its church-relatedness seriously. Faculty members will be encouraged to participate in religious activities and to share, where possible, their beliefs and value systems with students in contributing to their spiritual development.[6]

There can be no doubt, then, that Baylor's faculty throughout its first 125-or-so years was largely Baptist and overwhelmingly Christian. After all, Baylor was explicitly founded as a Baptist university, and in 1850 its charter was amended to provide for the naming of trustees by the Texas Baptist State Convention. Then, in 1851, the pastor of the one and only Baptist church in Houston, Rufus C. Burleson, became Baylor's second president. His appointment was indicative of the close relationship that existed and has continued to exist over the years between the church, the community of Baptist churches in particular, and the trustees, administrators, and faculty members of the university—a relationship of mutual support and faithfulness. Anecdotal evidence of the Baptist and Christian identity of faculty members can also be found in past issues of *The Baylor Bulletin*, where biographical paragraphs about new faculty members were included from time to time.

Nothing that might be described as a "mission statement" appeared in Baylor publications until 1936, then under the title "The Spirit and Purpose of Baylor University." However, a first step toward what would much later become Baylor's mission statement was taken as early as 1900 with the inclusion in the annual catalogue of a brief history of the university, describing its founding and other important developments and events, including the various presidencies, up to and through the move to Waco in 1886. As mission statements, variously called "The Aims of Baylor" or the "Purpose of Baylor University," became more and more prominent in Baylor catalogues, historical accounts of the university became less common. The term "Mission Statement" appeared for the first time in 1994 under the influence of the new guidelines for accreditation of the Southern Association of Colleges and Schools (SACS).

Although a declaration explicitly identified as a mission statement had only recently appeared in the catalogue, from the very beginning of Baylor's history the motto, *Pro Ecclesia, Pro Texana*, coined by Burleson during his first stint as Baylor president, and adopted for the seal of the university, appeared again and again in Baylor publications as reflecting Baylor's essential reason for being. Baylor was created to be of service to the church and to society. This meant for students an education that was primarily classical in nature and a campus life that was guided by high Christian ideals and moral practices. The catalogue of 1856 summarizes the latter goal clearly: "The government of the University is designed to partake both of a moral and parental character."[7] The *in loco parentis* role of the university was simply assumed.

While there was not an explicit Christian character to the general (non-ministerial) curriculum at Baylor for its first seventy-five years of existence, this fact should not be interpreted to mean that the university placed little emphasis on instruction in the Christian faith and doctrines. But with no such subjects required within the curriculum, how was this knowledge acquired? Though there were a few elective courses offered in such subjects as "Evidences of Christianity," "Biblical Literature," and "Ecclesiastical History," for example, the primary means through which students were taught about the Christian faith and its requirements were the daily chapel required of all students, voluntary Bible study, and required attendance at Sabbath schools and church every Sunday. Attendance at both chapel and church activities was considered as much Baylor's responsibility as regular class attendance. The integration of the Christian faith into one's total life as a student was taken for granted. No theory or philosophy of Christian higher education was needed; the practices of piety and a rigorous education were seen as clearly adequate for the task at hand.

Until the presidency of Samuel Palmer Brooks, from 1902 until his death in 1931, Baylor had been an undergraduate college. A product of both Baylor and Yale, Brooks created a number of new academic divisions that established the traditional elements of a true university. These included a College of Medicine, a School of Pharmacy, a Theological Seminary (which in a few years was separated from the University and moved to Fort Worth), a College of Dentistry, a School of Law (although a law program had existed earlier), a School of Business, and a School of Music, as well as the reorganization of the College of Arts and Sciences and the subsequent creation of a School of Education. In spite of these groundbreaking changes in the academic structure of the university, the traditional Christian and educational features of Baylor remained in place. *The Baylor Bulletin* of 1938-1939 indicated as much, since it included under the heading "General Information," a series of paragraphs that today might be called a mission statement:

> For nearly one hundred years . . . the institution has kept its doors open to ambitious student life around the world. While it is owned and controlled by the Baptists of Texas, it is maintained for the benefit of all mankind. It is not carried on in order that the dogmas of the denomination may be proclaimed, but that therein may be taught with religious fervor and flavor all things properly embodied in the curriculum of a great university.
>
> . . . No university can be great, whatever may be its assets, whatever may be its scholastic achievements, that does not develop within its own life a pure, radiant, institutional soul. "It is the spirit that giveth life; the flesh profiteth nothing."
>
> The thing of superlative importance about any university is its atmosphere. At least sixty per cent of all college culture is atmospheric. What is taught is not as important as the atmosphere in which it is taught. The atmosphere of Baylor University, like the atmosphere of the earth, is a mixture of life-giving components. It is calm with culture, warm with human sympathy, electric with inspiration, vibrant with intellectual health, and dynamic with the ideals of the Christian religion.
>
> The highest purpose of Baylor University is to develop men and women of Christian culture and character. Throughout its history of nearly one hundred years, it has accepted the high responsibility of training the youth of the land for service to church and state. It breathes at all times the spirit of its motto, "Pro Ecclesia, Pro Texana."[8]

Some of these themes are noted by C. E. Bryant, Director of Public Relations for Baylor, in the *Encyclopedia of Southern Baptists* published in 1958: "Christian principles dominate the Baylor campus, in the classroom and out. Faculty members are employed after careful consideration of religious belief and practice. All freshmen and sophomore students meet three times weekly for religious services in the university chapel. Students conduct the Baylor Religious Hour to which hundreds come voluntarily for worship each Wednesday evening. Devotional services are held on the campus each morning and at noon on school days."[9] *The Baylor Bulletin* of 1965-1966 explained the purpose of Baylor in this fashion:

> As a Christian institution, the University strives to integrate the essence of the Christian faith in its whole process of education. The University attempts continually to stimulate free inquiry for truth in a Christian atmosphere. The ideal objective of its educational process is a cultured person, equipped intellectually, socially, and religiously to serve God as a free and responsible citizen in all private and public pursuits. The University expects her graduates to become leaders, as well as participants, in both church and state, for her motto is Pro Ecclesia, Pro Texana.[10]

The point of this brief overview of the first 125 years of Baylor's history is to show that while Baylor had a clear, consistent, and compelling vision stated succinctly in its motto *Pro Ecclesia, Pro Texana*, the understanding and enactment of that vision was not grounded in a philosophy of Christian higher education on the order of Newman's lectures, but rather was based on a set of beliefs and practices that seemed patently obvious for the establishment and maintenance of a Christian institution of higher education in Texas. Baylor's founding and perpetuation were based on the common sense of Baptist Christians, not on theory. And the reason it worked, in addition to the guiding providential hand of God, was that there was a broad consensus among the people of Baylor and its supporters on all the major issues—whether in its founding need and purposes, its leadership (though there were quarrels at times), its curriculum, its faculty, its academic and behavioral requirements for students, its relationship to Baptists, to local Baptist congregations, and to other denominational churches, or its expected contribution to the good of a democratic society. Yes, there were controversies—some serious, such as whether or not to create a separate "Female College" or how to respond to charges brought by J. Frank Norris, pastor of the First Baptist Church in Fort Worth, that Baylor faculty members were "disavowing Biblical truths and were promoting Darwinian evolution."[11] Others were not so serious, such as whether or not to participate in intercollegiate athletics and particularly whether to play football, or how to set the seating rules in chapel. Yet through all of these controversies, the Baylor consensus about its nature, purposes, and practices was strong and essentially unchanging.

II

In the late 1960s and the early 1970s the broad consensus that had enveloped Baylor for the first 125 years of its history, though unnoticed at the time, began to undergo lasting fissures. The causes of this cracking of the consensus, as well as their consequences, remain with us today as we think about and plan for Baylor's future, particularly as expressed in the Baylor 2012 vision issued by President Robert B. Sloan in 2001. Furthermore, because these fissures throw into question any claim of a clear consensus regarding Baylor's beliefs and practices, Baylor needs to develop a unifying philosophy of Christian higher education, one that can help to answer two questions. First, what does it mean to be a preeminent Christian university in the Baptist tradition? Second, what are the grounds for such meaning? Ideas regarding these questions now matter as never before, precisely because Baylor people no longer share fundamental agreement on what Baylor ought to be. Recent essays in both the *Baylor Line* and the *Baylor Magazine*, as well as articles published elsewhere, demonstrate the current "struggle for the soul of Baylor." In addition, I believe that the great interest on the part of the faculty and the administration of Baylor in the colloquy, "The Baptist and Christian Character of Baylor," from which this publication has resulted, was due in large part to their felt need to argue back to first principles about what it means and does not mean to be a Christian university; about what such meanings might or might not imply with regard to faculty hiring, tenure, and promotion; and about what such meanings might or might not imply regarding Baylor's mission as both a religious and an intellectual community.

What were the causes of the crumbling of the Baylor consensus that first began to appear in the late 1960s? Among many others, these are primary: the protest movement of American youth in the 1960s and early 1970s, broadly affecting the lifestyle of most university students; the emerging culture of relativism and personal preference, granting an increasing weight to individual interests over institutional interests; the gradual withdrawal by Baylor from responsibility for the residential life of all but freshman students; the secularization of research universities across the United States and its impact on the recruitment of new faculty members to Christian colleges and universities; the reappearance of a strong fundamentalist movement in the Southern Baptist Convention having the stated aim of the movement's leaders to control Baylor; the decreasing interest in denominational affiliation across America and the loss of influence on Baylor students of the established Baptist churches of Waco; the Baylor charter change in 1990-1991; Baylor's entry into the Big 12 athletic conference and the creation of a new set of peer universities, all national research institutions; the emphasis in the 1990s on the integration of faith and learning; the uncertainties surrounding the selection of a new Baylor president to succeed Herbert H. Reynolds; the higher standards for both the religious and academic qualifications of faculty members in hiring and tenure; and the new emphasis over the last decade on graduate education, faculty research and publications, as well as grantsmanship and funded research.

Undoubtedly, the watershed event of the post-1960s era was the charter change initiated in September 1990 and consummated at the annual meeting of Baptist General Convention of Texas (BGCT) in November 1991. This action, led by then-President Reynolds and approved by the Board of Trustees—now called the Board of Regents—and ratified by the BGCT, reflected a break with the past that represented potentially, at least, a point of new beginning for Baylor. It is critical to remember that the context for the charter change was the struggle then taking place within the Southern Baptist Convention (SBC) over the control of the denomination's institutions and agencies. This struggle had its beginnings in the 1970s, and when in 1979 the SBC elected as its new president, an avowed fundamentalist leader, the process was set in motion to change the leadership of every SBC institution and agency. All six SBC seminaries experienced such fundamentalist control over the next fifteen years, as did the major SBC agencies, such as the boards for foreign missions and home missions. The next big target was Baylor, the "crown jewel" of state Baptist institutions. This was a family feud, for Baylor presidents and graduates over the years had occupied positions of enormous leadership and influence in the SBC, including the presidency, top administrative positions in various institutions and agencies, and major pastorates. Nevertheless, during the 1980s the religion department at Baylor, along with some other individual faculty members, was attacked for not adhering to a view of Scripture that satisfied the inerrantist views of the fundamentalists. Furthermore, a handful of such fundamentalists had been appointed to the Board of Trustees of Baylor, not only creating friction in the Board, but also serving as a conduit for transmitting allegations against Baylor faculty members to the new SBC national leadership.

In a strategic move worthy of any highly skilled military leader, then-President Reynolds led a legal takeover of the Baylor Board that secured the university's independence from the hostile forces of the far right—namely, the political fundamentalists of the SBC. The university's new charter called for a largely self-perpetuating Board, one that would remain totally Baptist, but which could now be national in make-up. In addition, the word "Southern" was taken out of all official documents that referred to the Baptist identity of Baylor. Most important of all, however, was the opportunity for Baylor to reflect on its Baptist and Christian character as a university. Some commentators believed that the charter change would mean that Baylor would soon go the way of Wake Forest, Richmond, and the major church-affiliated universities founded in the nineteenth century by the Methodists. Such an outcome was, indeed, a possibility, but it did not occur. Instead, the new freedom secured for Baylor was used to strengthen the religious underpinnings of the university, underpinnings that had been threatened by three decades of uncertainty.

In fact, what has happened at Baylor since the charter change has been, in a sense, a protracted discussion of the question, What does it mean to be a Christian university in the Baptist tradition? This discussion has taken place in the context of institutional freedom, on the one hand, but in the absence of any formal Baptist doctrine or theory of higher education, on the other. At the same time, the discussion has taken place with the benefit of more than a century of inherited practices. The inherited definition of Baylor as a Christian university, expressed eloquently in *The Baylor Bulletin* of 1938-1939 and reflected in the rhetoric of Baylor's leadership and in its publications into the 1990s, was based on the "atmospheric" model,[12] a view of the Christian university defined largely by its student life, placing emphasis on a highly moral and religious kind of campus culture as its major ingredient. A common way of expressing Baylor's purpose, under this model, was to say that Baylor offered an excellent education in a "Christian environment." Abner V. McCall, as Chancellor, argued for such a view in the February 1985 edition of the *Baylor Line*. He wrote: "The description 'Christian' should imply that all who operate our [educational] institutions should strive to give the quality of excellence. . . . Further, when we designate our institutions as 'Christian,' we profess that their services are rendered in a Christian manner—with respect, concern, compassion, and love for those serving and those served."[13]

The large question left unanswered by the atmospheric model was the relationship of the Christian faith to the central part of the university, its intellectual life. This is not to say that this question had never been addressed at Baylor. After all, one aspect of the moral and religious atmosphere of the university was its academic life. Discussions between faculty members and students, and between students and students, regarding religion and intellectual issues were as common as eating meals. Furthermore, *The Baylor Bulletin* as early as 1965-1966 includes in its purpose statement a clear mandate to connect the Christian faith to all of university life: "As a Christian institution, the University strives to integrate the essence of the Christian faith in its whole process of education."[14] It was not until the 1990s, however, that the "integration" model began to supplement, if not supplant, the atmospheric model. The integration model holds that it is a necessary condition of a Christian university that it bring the resources of the Christian faith to bear on the essence of what a university is—namely, its entire intellectual life and discourse. The presumption is that the Christian faith—in its scripture, traditions, and theology—contains essential knowledge and wisdom that bring enlightenment and understanding to all other forms of learning. A Christian atmosphere is important, but atmosphere alone does not make a university a Christian university in the most basic and relevant sense.

Indeed, several scholars have argued that the absence of some version of this integration model has led to the demise of many formerly Christian colleges and universities. If the Christian faith is not relevant to the academic enterprise, the latter comes totally under the dominance of secular learning and its God-denying assumptions about the world. A Christian atmosphere, as important as it is in the ethos of an institution, cannot by itself withstand the overwhelming onslaught of academic secularization. Following an all-too-familiar pattern, the Christian college or university which does not integrate faith and learning will eventually collapse from within.

That such an outcome is likely has been demonstrated by the evidence garnered by several important scholars over the last ten years or so. For example, George Marsden, in his account of secularizing tendencies from pre-revolutionary America to the twentieth century (*The Soul of the American University*, 1994), points to the inherent weaknesses of building Christian higher education upon the basis of the churches' cultural hegemony rather than the intellectual substance of the Christian faith itself. Marsden explains that the demise of a predominantly Christian culture over the last two centuries has prompted numerous Christian colleges and universities to abandon their Christian identity and to become secularized. Other significant studies affirm the essential features of Marsden's narrative and have done so across denominational lines, within varied institutional settings, and throughout widely varied regions of the country (e.g., see Douglas Sloan, *Faith and Knowledge*, 1994; Philip Gleason, *Contending With Modernity*, 1996; and James Burtchaell, *The Dying of the Light*, 1998). Given the trajectory of the past, these scholars share a genuine apprehension about the future of Christian higher education. To put the matter plainly, history shows that following the atmospheric model at the university level leads, without exception, to a secular university.

This broader concern about Christian higher education is another important component of the context today in which we at Baylor are attempting to sort out what it means to be a preeminent Christian university in the Baptist tradition. At the same time we must also address the attendant concerns not only of faculty hiring, tenure, and promotion, but also of the relationship of the mission of Baylor to our academic goals, including research, on the one hand, and to Baptists and the larger Christian community, on the other. What appears in this book is our attempt to explore these issues—to offer Newman-like reflections on the nature of a Christian university and, in light of these reflections, to examine the various implications these issues have for our institutional life. Some might say that the colloquy on "The Baptist and Christian Character of Baylor" should have come sooner, perhaps prior to the creation of Baylor 2012. But institutions, like individuals and all life, have their seasons of readiness. The colloquy was important in April 2003 because there was then and is now a widespread desire to come together as a community to speak openly and freely about what it means to be a Christian university in the Baptist tradition and to think about what the future of Baylor ought to be.

III

This volume includes six major essays, five with responses, that constituted the core lectures of the colloquy on "The Baptist and Christian Character of Baylor." C. Stephen Evans offers a persuasive account of how we might understand a Christian university in the present age. Drawing on Newman's work, *The Idea of a University*, Evans argues that the "connectedness of knowledge" in the university depends on the presence and interrelation of all major areas of knowledge, including theology. If theology is removed from the university, then the whole structure of what is known is incomplete and thereby harmed. This concept of the connectedness of knowledge is, however, a contested idea in the contemporary university setting and leads, appropriately, to contested ideas about the nature of the university. Within the context of a diversity of universities, the Christian university surely has a legitimate place, indeed, a particularly valuable place within the contours of American higher education. Evans elaborates on some of the characteristics that are essential components of a university shaped by its commitment to "the grand Christian story," such as interdisciplinary thinking, moral and theological education, scholarship influenced by the Christian narrative, and Christian community. In a word, it is a university in which knowledge, in both its created and disseminated forms, is understood as a connected whole for those who, in faith, are convinced that the Christian narrative is true.

The next two essays consider the implications of being a serious Baptist and Christian university for faculty hiring, tenure, and promotion and offer compelling opposing arguments. In the first, Mikeal C. Parsons notes some important distinctions between the words "Baptist" and "Christian" as applied to a university. The word "Baptist" in this context suggests matters of religious style, such as freedom of conscience and non-creedalism. The word "Christian," on the other hand, points to matters of religious substance which are common to all Christian denominations, including Baptists, such as belief in the One Triune God and the efficacy of Christ's death and resurrection for sinful human beings. At Baylor, Parsons contends, both traditions are applied together and in some tension. This leads him to an exploration of and advocacy for a "Significant Contribution Model" in faculty hiring, tenure, and promotion at Baylor. Parsons argues that faculty members should be hired and evaluated, in part, with a clear estimation of their potential or actual contribution to the

Baptist and Christian character of Baylor. Parsons shows not only that this model is tacitly in place at Baylor today, but also that there are important reasons to favor such a model. The task ahead, he points out, is to make clear the expectations of this model.

In contrast to Parsons, Robert M. Baird advocates a more fluid set of boundaries than those currently in place for religious requirements in hiring, tenuring, and promotion of Baylor faculty members. Drawing on his own experience at Baylor as both a student and a professor, Baird is persuaded that there is no reason to be anxious about Baylor's capacity to sustain its vibrant religious identity. He argues, therefore, that we should proceed with as much self-confidence about who we are as a Baptist and Christian university, as does a Catholic university, such as Notre Dame, and that to enrich the intellectual life of the university we should be willing to hire and tenure some faculty members who may not be "vigorous in the life of faith," or who, in some cases, may be of other religions altogether. He uses three examples to make his case: Haywood Shuford, the influential philosophy teacher while Baird was a student at Baylor; Charles Hartshorne, the renowned metaphysician and philosopher of religion; and Michael Ruse, an important philosopher of science and a recent lecturer on the Baylor campus. Baird contends that notwithstanding the value these three individuals might bring to the intellectual life of Baylor, none of them, given their own spiritual perspectives, would likely be hired today because of what he calls "this intense emphasis on the religious criterion." While acknowledging the risks that such faculty hires might impose, Baird concludes by advocating "a more open hiring policy."

The final two essays address issues involving the mission of Baylor, particularly in relation to our research emphasis and to questions dealing with the appropriate connections between the church and the life of Baylor. In "The Convergence of Research and Institutional Mission: A Faculty Perspective," Owen Lind traces the evolution of research and scholarly expectations of Baylor faculty members over the past forty years, roughly the timeframe of Lind's career at Baylor. He notes three distinct phases in the evolutionary process: the McCall years, a period when research was neglected; the Reynolds years, a period when research was encouraged; and the Sloan years, a period when research has become a requirement. Lind applauds the Sloan years, excited that his own calling as a research scientist and the Baylor 2012 vision for scholarship have finally met in their "converging journeys." However, Lind argues that, given the anti-religious bias in most scientific fields, if we are to be successful in achieving the aspirations of our vision, the religious requirements for hiring, especially as applied to scientists, need to be somewhat relaxed, without our abandoning the worthy goal of "building a world-class community of scholars who are Christian."

Ralph Wood's essay takes up the issue of Baylor's mission as a Christian university and the attendant obligations of both faculty members and the university administration. Wood contends that there is nothing to fear in the university's requirement that faculty members should belong to a local church because in the church, rightly understood as the Body of Christ, we find "Truth large enough to ground and inspire and direct our entire academic life, and Community large enough to include everyone except those who refuse to enter it." It must be remembered, Wood explains, that this notion of the "church catholic" finds its expression in the "church specific," the local congregation. Therefore, our capacity to be a Christian university and to be Christian scholars is directly related to vital church membership, where our corporate and individual work comes under the critique of the Word of God as enacted and proclaimed primarily in worship, but in other venues as well. We hear in the church a message of sin and redemption that plumbs the depths of human understanding and experience far beyond that of our academic disciplines.

What are the obligations of the administration? Wood argues that the university should seek to serve "the Kingdom of God in its largest ecumenical reach, not in any parochial sense." While maintaining our strengths as Baptists, we must at the same time embrace the larger Christian body and become "an ever-more ecumenically Christian university." This more ecumenical dimension should be reflected in those who are invited to teach in the Religion Department, in the sculpture exhibited on campus, and in a more liturgical form of worship in chapel. The latter, Wood contends, would be greatly enhanced with a new cathedral-like sanctuary located in the center of the campus.

* * * *

What these essays—as well as the various responses to them—collectively reveal is what I have stressed throughout this introduction: While there was an overwhelming consensus regarding the Baptist and Christian character of Baylor for its first approximately 125 years, this tacit agreement is now being seriously challenged. In fact, it has been tested from the 1970s onwards. The earlier consensus was based on a set of practices, grounded in sincere Christian piety, that was rarely, if ever, questioned. But once the "questioning" began, in all its cultural, religious, intellectual, and institutional manifestations, the consensus could no longer hold. In times such as these, ideas begin to matter as never before, hence the prolonged discussion during the decade of the 1990s on the meaning of Baylor as a Christian university. Would it be possible to arrive at some fundamental beliefs about Baylor's identity? Substantial progress emerged in this regard in 1994 with the approval, by the Board of Regents, of a new mission statement created during the 1994-1996 SACS self-study, probably the strongest overall mission document Baylor has ever had. In most respects, Baylor 2012 is based on the spirit of that mission statement, except for one all-important component: the goal that Baylor should become a top-tier Christian research university. While that language is not explicitly used in Baylor 2012, it is certainly implicit in it.

The 1994 mission statement, the Baylor 2012 vision document, and the recent colloquy on "The Baptist and Christian Character of Baylor," along with many other developments here at Baylor over the last two decades, demonstrate a new sense of intentionality about Baylor's direction for the future. No longer can matters surrounding Baylor's identity be taken for granted. Those institutions who have taken their religious identity for granted now either have no religious identity at all or have a religious identity that amounts to nothing more than an acknowledgement of the institution's "religious heritage." The good news for Baylor is that we are being intentional about our future as a preeminent Baptist and Christian university. The colloquy of April 10-11, 2003, was a grand and successful conversation about a contested idea, the meaning of a Christian university and its role in the landscape of American higher education.*

Notes

---

[1] Eugene W. Baker, *To Light the Ways of Time* (Waco, TX. Baylor University Press, 1987) 7.

[2] James Huckins was a Brown graduate and William M. Tryon was a Mercer graduate.

[3] Baker 56.

[4] *Annual Catalogue of Baylor University*, 1856, 19.

[5] Program and Administrative Survey, Volume 3, Christian Education Program, Baptist General Convention of Texas (1959) 99.
[6] Report of the Long-Range Plans Review Committee, to the Board of Trustees, Baylor University, January 19, 1978, 3.
[7] *Annual Catalogue of Baylor University*, 1856, 19.
[8] *The Baylor Bulletin*, 1938-1939, 24-25.
[9] *Encyclopedia of Southern Baptists*, Vol. I, 1958 ed.
[10] *Baylor University Bulletin*, 1965-1966, 3.
[11] Baker 133.
[12] *The Baylor Bulletin*, 1938-1939, 24.
[13] Abner V. McCall, "Why Baylor?" *The Baylor Line,* Feb 1985:12.
[14] *Baylor University Bulletin*, 1965-1966, 3.

* I wish to thank Ellen Brown and the staff of the Texas Collection for their generous assistance in my research for this essay.

Part One

*A University in the Largest Sense
of the Word*

Chapter 2

The Christian University and the Connectedness of Knowledge

C. Stephen Evans

I am very honored to be invited to be the first speaker at this colloquy in honor of Donald Schmeltekopf. Don's vision as Provost certainly is a large part of the reason why Baylor has undertaken both to raise its academic quality and deepen its Christian character. Of course, Don recruited me personally, and I feel a deep sense of gratitude for his confidence and trust in inviting me to play a role in the exciting adventure upon which Baylor has embarked.

I was asked to speak on the idea of a Christian university as a "university in the largest sense of the word." I am tempted to say that this is easily done. Simply locate the Christian university in Texas and surely size will be no problem, since everything in Texas is alleged to be larger than life. And Baylor has for many years claimed to be the world's largest Baptist university. Presumably, however, the idea behind the requested topic has nothing to do with physical size, or even the size of the student body, much less the size of the football team's offensive line, but rather connotes the idea of an expansive intellectual community. Can a Christian university be one that fulfills Newman's ideal of the university as a place for "teaching universal knowledge?"[1] Will not the adjective "Christian" inevitably constrict a university, so that the knowledge taught in such an institution cannot be genuinely universal?

I want to argue today that a Christian university can indeed be a genuine university, and that its Christian character is an asset and not a liability in its quest to achieve its goals. The most important reason why this is so is that a Christian university is ideally positioned to

21

pursue what I shall call the connectedness of knowledge. My case will build on elements of Newman's classic argument in *The Idea of a University*, but I will also diverge from Newman at certain key points.

Newman's Case for Christianity in the University

As I read Newman, he is not really defending the idea of a Christian university in the sense in which we might distinguish a Christian university from what we in the United States would call a public, secular university. The essence of the university for Newman is something that makes the university independent of the Church. To use Catholic language, one might say that the university has its home in the order of nature and not grace. However, in typical Catholic fashion, Newman thinks, with Aquinas, that grace presupposes nature and perfects it. To look at the matter from the other end, this implies that nature needs grace to be all that it can be, and thus, though the idea of the university is not directly linked to the Church, the university needs the "assistance" of the Church to fulfill its own mission.[2] Newman thus defends, not the idea of a Christian university in contradistinction from other kinds, but the claim that the public university is a better, one might say truer, university if it has a Christian character.

Someone might object to this reading of Newman on the grounds that Newman was, after all, making a case for a Catholic university in Dublin, and thus must have had a conception of a Catholic university as having a distinctive character. This is in one sense undoubtedly correct; Newman would certainly not have believed that the character of a Catholic university would be indistinguishable from its secular counterpart. He surely believed that the presence of Christian faculty and even Christian symbols would make important differences to a university. However, a close look at Newman's argument will show that his case for a Christian and Catholic university is rooted mainly in the claim that such a university will do a better job of fulfilling the aims of the university than is actually the case for a secular university. The aims of the university, for Newman, are essentially the same for any institution that aspires to be a true university.

One might think that the claim that universities should have a Christian character would be a non-starter in a pluralistic democracy today, especially with regard to state-supported universities, at least in a country such as the United States that has a tradition of the separation of church and state. Essentially, I think this claim is correct today; there is no realistic possibility that the contemporary secular university will regain any Christian character, even if this were thought to be desirable. However, it is instructive to see how recent is this way of thinking. As late as 1890 twenty-two of twenty-four state universities in the United States polled by the University of Michigan had daily chapel services sponsored by the institution, and at twelve of those institutions, attendance was mandatory.[3] In 1887, James B. Angell, the president of the University of Michigan, the leading state university of the time, explained why he would not be willing to hire a non-Christian for the history department: "In the Chair of History the work may lie and often does lie so close to Ethics, that I should not wish a pessimist or an agnostic or a man disposed to obtrude criticisms of Christian views of humanity or of Christian principles. I should not want a man who would not make historical judgments and interpretations from a Christian standpoint."[4] I cite these facts not to claim that we can or should turn back the clock to the days when America's public universities were essentially non-sectarian but Protestant institutions, but simply to show that a little more than a century ago Newman's assumption that a university could be both public and Christian was widely accepted in the United States, not just in a country such as England with an established Church.

Why is it that Newman, and very likely President Angell and others who thought as they did, could believe that the public university could and should be Christian?[5] Why is it that such a view would not be taken seriously at any major secular university today, public or private? What has changed? The answer, I think, lies in Newman's view that Christianity provides genuine knowledge. If the university seeks to transmit knowledge, and Christianity includes genuine knowledge, then Christianity must find a place in the university. Newman doubtless knew that even in his day he was swimming against the tide, but he nonetheless maintained that "[r]eligious doctrine is knowledge, in as full a sense as Newton's doctrine is knowledge. University Teaching without Theology is simply unphilosophical. Theology has at least as good a right to claim a place there as Astronomy."[6]

I take it then that part of what Newman means by insisting that Christianity be given a place in the university is that Christian theology should be given a place. If we "withdraw Theology from the public schools" the effect will be "to impair the completeness and to invalidate the trustworthiness of all that is actually taught in them."[7] However, on Newman's view, the university needs to do more than simply include theology among the subjects to be taught. This is because on Newman's view the sciences have a real unity: "If you drop any science out of the circle of knowledge, you cannot keep its place vacant for it; that science is forgotten; the other sciences close up, or, in other words, they exceed their proper bounds, and intrude where they have no right."[8] Since the sciences (and I think Newman means by the "sciences" *Wissenschaften*, all the learned disciplines, not merely the natural and social sciences) form a natural unity, to withdraw one science is to impair the whole. Theology is naturally and organically linked to the other sciences in such a way that if it drops out, they are harmed as well.

If I am right in my reading of Newman, then it is perfectly clear why Newman's vision of the university is no longer a viable intellectual force at our leading universities. For very few people at such universities share Newman's confidence that theology gives us genuine knowledge, knowledge on a par with astronomy. In fact, a careful reading of Newman's *The Idea of a University* shows that this was already increasingly true in Newman's day; Newman recognizes that he is fighting a battle against views that increasingly relegated theology to some other category than knowledge.[9] Today, if theology is tolerated at all as a respectable enterprise, it is thought to be rooted in something other than knowledge: theology is rooted in or gives birth to faith, values, emotions, existential commitments, or fundamental attitudes—anything but knowledge.

Newman's other assumption, that knowledge forms a natural unity such that the loss of one discipline would necessarily impoverish the whole, is also not widely shared today. Scholars are certainly open to the idea that there are connections between particular areas of inquiry. Psychologists who study motivation might conceivably learn something of interest to economists; economists who study preferential behavior might have something to offer psychologists. In the natural sciences there are programs to integrate chemistry and biology, physics and chemistry, neurophysiology and psychology. However, most scholars take for granted that knowledge, with the exception of the kind of particular relations mentioned, is specialized and fragmented. This is so even within a field. Historians of ancient China will not as a general rule find themselves crippled if there are no good historians studying colonial America within earshot. Art historians will not find their work severely impaired if there are no symbolic logicians around. Rather, various disciplines can flourish or flounder, wax or wane, without necessarily having much impact on others, unless those others are close neighbors.

In such an environment, the suggestion that physicists, economists, and logicians will be significantly harmed if theology is not present in the academy can only be regarded as quaint, and doubtless that is how such a suggestion would be viewed if someone were bold enough to make it at Stanford or Berkeley. Few people would be prepared to grant that theology is a source of genuine knowledge; that is why major universities typically have "religious studies" departments which view religions as objects to be studied rather than sources of knowledge. However, even if theology were regarded as a source of knowledge, hardly anyone believes that the whole of knowledge forms an ordered edifice such that the entire building is severely harmed if one section of the structure is missing.

I do not think, therefore, that the case for Christianity in the contemporary university can simply build on Newman. We cannot make a convincing argument that all universities need the assistance of Christian faith to be genuine universities. However, we can, I think, make a powerful argument that a Christian university is a legitimate ideal, and that a Christian university has a special and valuable contribution to make to the contemporary educational community in North America. I shall try to show that a Christian university as I understand it is in an excellent position to realize the goals of the university as Newman conceives it. Perhaps a case can be made that it is better positioned to do so than any other kind of university. However, other types of universities may dispute this claim and argue that they are equally well-positioned to achieve these goals. The university as I shall describe it is thus a contested ideal, existing in a plurality of forms.

It might appear that my argument, when compared with Newman's, concedes too much to the secular university. In arguing for the validity and value of the Christian university, I am implicitly conceding the legitimacy, and perhaps the value, of the non-Christian university as well. However, the argument I shall present does not appear to me as second-best at all. Newman's argument, if viable, fits a society with an established church very well, whether that church be established *de jure*, as in the United Kingdom, or merely *de facto*, as was the case in nineteenth-century American public universities that were effectively Protestant schools. The argument I shall present, however, strikes me as entirely fitting for a Baptist university, since

Baptists have historically been opposed to the establishment of any church, and welcome the pluralism that freedom from state control provides. Baptists have no desire that all universities should be Baptist, or Christian, or even religious in character. A pluralistic system of education is welcome not because Christianity no longer plays a culturally dominant role, but because of the demands of faith itself. A defense of a Christian university as one valid form for the contemporary university is thus an especially fitting one if the Christian university in question is Baptist.

The Christian University: Pluralistic Models or a Coherent Ideal?

One might think that the variety of Christian institutions of higher education makes it impossible to describe the Christian university as rooted in a coherent ideal. This is at least the lesson that some might draw from my friend Richard Hughes' recent book, *How Christian Faith Can Sustain the Life of the Mind*.[10] Hughes, building on the work embedded in his co-edited volume, *Models for Christian Higher Education*, focuses on what is distinctive about various Christian denominational traditions and the implications of this distinctiveness for Christian institutions of higher education. Catholics, Lutherans, Wesleyans, Calvinists, and Anabaptists all offer us particular models of Christian higher education.[11]

As Hughes tells the story, for example, Reformed (Calvinist) Christians put the sovereignty of God at the center of their theological vision, and this emphasis leads to a focus on the rule of God over every aspect of life. This in turn implies the characteristically Reformed emphasis on the development of distinctively Christian perspectives on the various academic disciplines, on the arts, and on society, all as part of a comprehensive "Christian world-view."[12]

This Reformed model, as Hughes tells the story, differs in several ways from the models of Christian higher education offered by others. Mennonites, for example, put their emphasis primarily on the notion of radical discipleship, and from this perspective the Reformed stress on a "Christian world and life view" is "cerebral."[13] The Mennonite model, in contrast, puts a great deal of emphasis on selfless service and the ways in which thinking is reshaped by living in a distinctive way. Catholic theology, says Hughes, tends to be fundamentally "incarnational and sacramental," and this enables Catholics to "find the grace of God displayed in actions and events that a variety of Protestants, especially in the Reformed tradition, might find altogether secular."[14]   Lutherans, avers Hughes, also have their characteristic theological vision, centered on the idea of a "dialectical tension" between "the kingdom of grace" and the "kingdom of nature," leading to their own model of Christian higher education.

Hughes' work is clearly very valuable in highlighting the diversity that actually exists in Christian higher education. And he is clearly right to suggest that some of this diversity can be traced to characteristic theological differences that can be seen in various denominational traditions. However, I want to argue that we draw the wrong conclusion from these findings if we think that there is no unified ideal of Christian higher education, but rather merely a collection of irreducibly different models from which we may choose or that we might syncretistically blend together. (I hasten to add that I am not suggesting that Hughes himself would draw such a conclusion.) The diversity in Christian higher education should not blind us to what makes all forms of Christian higher education Christian, just as the diversity of Christian denominations and theological distinctives should not obscure what Christians hold in common.

Hughes develops his models, as we have seen, by selecting one theological motif that he sees as characteristic or specially important for the tradition in question. Thus, Calvinists emphasize divine sovereignty, Anabaptists discipleship, Lutherans the tension between sin and grace. However, as Hughes himself admits, but as an unwary reader might not notice, each theme that is attributed to a particular tradition is present in some form in each of the other traditions. It would be a fundamental error to think that only Reformed Christians, and not Catholics or Lutherans or Anabaptists, are concerned with divine sovereignty and the kingdom of God. One would be equally mistaken to think that Reformed Christians care only about God's rule over the intellect and have no concern for discipleship or putting faith into action, or that Catholics have no appreciation for the seriousness of sin and the need for grace.

It would be an error to think, for example, that because Reformed Christians have written at length about the need for the development of a Christian world and life view, a Reformed college will be overly "cerebral" and unconcerned about the practical implications of Christianity. This is far from the case; Calvin College, for example, is a national leader among all colleges, and probably the leading Christian institution, in the development of "service-learning," in which practical service is integrated into the educational curriculum.

Or, one might think that because Mennonites have emphasized the importance of practical service, they would have less concern for a Christian critique of the intellectual foundations of the disciplines. However, I have two friends who are Mennonite economists who are profoundly concerned about the question as to how the standard model employed by economics relates to Christian thinking about the nature of the human person.

Hughes is correct to say that particular theological themes are specially emphasized by certain traditions.   And there are also significant differences in the way particular themes are developed by the various traditions.   Reformed Christians and Mennonites may be equally concerned with discipleship, but they have different understandings of what radical discipleship implies for Christians striving to be faithful to God.   However, these differences must not obscure the fact that all of the themes emphasized and developed in different ways by the various traditions are taken from something that all the historic Christian traditions share in common.

What is this common heritage?   It is not, I think, best understood as a set of doctrines, though various doctrines are probably included or implied by this shared inheritance.   What the various streams of historic Christianity share is a common narrative, a grand drama with fundamental and pervasive themes, a compelling plot—replete with stunning twists and deep irony—significant characters, and a promised ending that surpasses our imaginative powers.   Like any good story, the action can be parsed in various ways, but I prefer to think that there are four main acts to the drama: creation, fall, redemption, and final victory.[15]   Of course, for Christians the drama is not fiction, but a true story, one played out on the stages of both heaven and the earth.

The premier agent in the story is the Triune God.   God the Father, God the Son, and God the Spirit are the three-in-one who create the universe out of nothing and continually sustain it.   They create humans in the image of God; thus the God who is in himself a social being creates humans as social creatures with a fundamental need to relate to God and to their fellow creatures.   Sadly, humans fail to relate properly to God and hence fail to relate properly to ourselves, our fellows, and the created order.   God, however, does not abandon his fallen creation, but begins a rescue plan by calling the ancient Hebrews to be a special people of God, a people to make known the goodness and mercy of God to all the nations.   God delivers his people from Egypt through mighty wonders and gives them a land of their own. The people of Israel are often unfaithful to their call, but God continues to send them judges and prophets to recall them to faithfulness. Finally, God sends to Israel and the world his own Son, Jesus of Nazareth, who is fully human and fully divine. The life, death, and resurrection of Jesus is the means whereby God offers salvation from sin and death to all humans, and creates a new people of God, the Church, a community sustained by the Spirit. The members of this community also have a calling from God, both collectively and as individuals. Jesus promises to return and usher in a final victory over evil; in the interim his people enjoy life with God through the Spirit. Even though the forces of evil appear still to be strong, God's people have confidence that the decisive battle has been fought and final victory is assured.

This summary of the story, like any plot summary, is of course highly condensed and selective, leaving out most of the power of the story. With respect to this story, it is literally true that "God is in the details." However, my task today does not allow more than a brief summary.

Christians are those who are committed to the Lordship of Jesus of Nazareth. Every Christian must see himself or herself as called by God to become a new creature in Christ. However, the identity of Jesus is only grasped when his story is seen as the central and decisive act in the wider story that I have been describing as the common heritage of Christians. Hence, Christians, through their commitment to Jesus, are also people who understand their lives in relation to this story. Since the story is of course the story told in the Bible taken as a whole, as interpreted by the Church, it is literally true that Christians are, as David Jeffrey has written, a "people of the book." It is this story that is the basis of what C. S. Lewis termed, following Richard Baxter, "mere Christianity." One might say that Christians cannot come to understand what they are called to be concretely except by way of relating their own lives—their personal stories—to the grand story that defines their faith.

I would argue that the central teachings or doctrines of Christianity are best understood as attempts to articulate the meaning of various aspects of this story. Thus, Christians can disagree about the exact nature of the atonement or creation precisely because they share a commitment to this story. The kinds of theological distinctives Hughes emphasizes thus point us back in a somewhat paradoxical way to an underlying unity.

This is why we can speak of the ideal of the Christian university and not simply of a disparate collection of models. The Christian university as I understand it is sustained by a community of people committed to this basic story as providing the ultimate framework for understanding themselves, their world, and God. Of course, no actual Christian university will be this ideal in abstraction; an actual university must be a concrete community and every such community will indeed have distinctive ways of understanding and interpreting the story. However, in the contemporary situation, in which Christian faith is an embattled intellectual tradition, it is crucial that Christians have a clear vision for what they have in common. A Christian university that focuses on this common Christian heritage will be an ecumenical community in precisely the way Baylor's 2012 Vision statement maintains; it will understand its particularity as a concrete expression of what all committed Christians hold in common.

There are many themes I could touch upon if I wished to speak about the particularities of a Baptist university. I could speak about the missionary urgency that Baptists have traditionally exhibited and ask whether this zeal can be wedded to the task of relating the gospel to the academy. I could speak about the importance of believer's baptism as a powerful expression of an understanding of the Church as a community of the Spirit that is created by God's actions and human responses, rather than a community that can be identified with some human social, ethnic, or national group. Such themes, however important, must not obscure the fundamental importance of what Baptists share with other Christians, and it is that common heritage that is my major subject.

The University as an Essentially Contested Good

In the concluding sections of this paper, I wish to try to say something about the nature of the Christian university that understands itself against the backdrop of this story. I want to argue that such a university is well-situated to fulfill Newman's understanding of the university as an institution that exists for the transmission of knowledge, where knowledge itself is understood as a connected whole. The biggest difference between my account and Newman's is that I do not share his modern (or pre-modern) assumption that the knowledge the university exists to transmit is an agreed-upon body of insight that is the common possession of scholars. Instead, my own conviction is that knowledge, in the contemporary world, is what I should call an essentially contested good. An essentially contested good is some good that is generally agreed to be vital to human flourishing, but about which there is a sustained argument, both with respect to the nature of this good and how it is to be attained.

Other essentially contested goods would include such notions as justice and perhaps even human happiness itself. Everyone is in favor of a just society, but there is deep disagreement as to whether, for example, a society with an inheritance tax is more or less just than one that has no such tax. Everyone wants happiness, but there is fundamental disagreement as to whether people are happier when they function as autonomous individuals who only regard relationships that are freely chosen as contributing to their happiness, or rather regard happiness as a function of familial and community ties that are central to a person's identity.

I take it that our postmodern situation is one in which knowledge is such a contested concept. This may not appear to be the case if we focus our attention largely on technical and scientific knowledge, where a fair amount of consensus still exists within various disciplines. However, even in the sciences the concept of "paradigms" and "scientific revolutions" has opened the eyes of philosophers of science to the ways science itself can be a contested notion. And if we turn our attention to the social sciences, the radical debates between "evolutionary" theorists such as Steven Pinker, who argue that huge amounts of human behavior are shaped by our DNA, and more "liberal" thinkers who hold that human behavior is more fundamentally plastic and open to shaping both by the environment and by individual choices, show that there are fundamental disagreements as to what counts as knowledge of human beings. The essentially contested character of knowledge is still more evident if we look at the fundamental disputes in philosophy, in literature, in art and music history, and above all in religion.

If Newman is right in thinking of the university as a place for the transmission (and, I would add, development) of knowledge, and if I am right in thinking that knowledge is an essentially contested ideal, then it follows that the university itself will be a contested ideal. Different universities will have somewhat different understandings of what counts as knowledge and how it is to be advanced and passed on. And this leads to the notion that a plurality of universities, as well as types of universities, is a good thing.

The ongoing and probably irresolvable disputes present in contemporary scholarship show that the notion of the scholar as a purely objective thinker who simply draws conclusions based on indisputable facts is naive. We do not have to react to this situation by going to the opposite extreme and denying that there are such things as facts or by ignoring the value of such intellectual virtues as honesty and a willingness to consider the problems that facts may pose for our theories. However, the radical disagreements within the contemporary university should teach us some intellectual humility. We must recognize that none of us is the embodiment of "pure reason." We are finite, historically situated creatures, and thus we must be open to the possibility that, for example, western philosophy exhibits racial and masculine bias. We can no longer pretend that the university is a place with a large sign over the entrance gate, proclaiming that those who enter must put on the identity of "rational knowers" and thereby forget whether they are male or female, European-American or African-American, religious or non-religious. Our basic values and convictions do shape the way we function as scholars, though, to be sure, this is less true for some areas of inquiry than others, more true for some kinds of questions than others. Contrary to what some may think, such a situation does not necessarily lead to a university where the quest for truth has been replaced by interest groups pursuing political agendas. Rather, we must reconceive the quest for truth as a pluralistic conversation, where no party to the conversation can claim to represent "pure reason."

It is because of this situation that so many universities and colleges today place a high value on diversity within the community. It is a good thing to have women as well as men, Hispanics as well as those of northern European ancestry, people of color as well as Caucasians, represented in the academy. The university is right to value this diversity. However, I would argue that diversity is not merely valuable within individual educational institutions but valuable within the system of higher education generally. It is a strength of American higher education that it includes state institutions, secular private institutions, and Catholic institutions. It is a good thing to have universities with social science departments vigorously pursuing a research agenda dominated by evolutionary theory and also a good thing to have schools with departments with competing research agendas. An outstanding research university that has a distinctively Protestant Christian character is the one missing piece from this mosaic, and it is this piece that Baylor is now endeavoring to supply. The contribution Baylor can make is a significant one, not only for the intrinsic value of what it can accomplish if it is true to its vision, but for the example it will set to the many church-related institutions that are currently uncertain as to how to maintain their identity.

Can a school that is committed to Christian education be one that exists to transmit "universal knowledge?" If we mean by universal knowledge something that is acquired and transmitted by pure reason, unfettered by commitments and free from all particularities, the answer is no. However, this is impossible not merely for the Christian university but for every university. None of us humans sees the world *sub specie æternitatis*. It is clear that this is not what Newman himself meant by the phrase. Rather, in speaking of "universal knowledge" Newman meant to claim that the university must not regard any subject matter or question as out of bounds. He meant that the scope of inquiry should be universal and not that the inquirers could be free from their particularities. In this sense of universal knowledge, the Christian university can certainly strive to be a place for open and unfettered inquiry.

The Character and Contributions of a Christian University

I have argued that a Christian university is one that is shaped by the commitment of the community that constitutes that university to what I call the grand Christian story. This community is one that tries to understand itself and everything else in the context of this basic narrative. From this narrative they gain a sense of what has value and what has meaning, a sense of the purposes of human life and the purposes of the university itself. Such a university is a contested ideal because its grounding narrative is, in today's world and perhaps in any world short of the eschaton, also contested. We can, in fact, think of the Christian story in the terms of theologian James McLendon, who uses the image of a "tournament of narratives," in which the Christian story must preserve its integrity as it competes with other master-narratives.[16] What would a university that is shaped by such a narrative look like?

Let me begin this concluding part of my tale by sketching some characteristics that are necessary elements of such a university but which are not sufficient taken alone. The first such element is that the community that constitutes a Christian university must constitute a genuinely Christian community. This in itself has many profound implications. The community must deal with its members and with the wider society of which it is a part in ways characterized by love and justice. Opportunities for common worship and spiritual development should be provided for all. Every aspect of the community, from compensation philosophy and hiring practices to grading practices and athletic policies, should be examined to determine whether it fits with Christian principles and contributes to the development of Christian community. Students must always be viewed as persons made in God's image as well as people for whom Christ died. Each member of the community should model for the students and others those virtues which stem from being united to God in Christ. One might say that by virtue of this realization of Christian community the context in which education and research will take place will be a Christian one.

I do not think that the Christian university can realize its essence merely by virtue of the fact that a Christian context is provided for education. Such a goal is important, but it leaves the most important business of the university—teaching and research—externally related to the Christian character of the university. People who understand their whole lives and their callings in relation to the basic Christian narrative can hardly be content to leave their work as scholars as something unrelated to that story, at least if we agree that this work is an important part of their callings.

One might think then that what must be added to the Christian community that provides a context for education is moral and theological education. Perhaps the Christian university, in addition to providing a Christian community in which education occurs, differs from a secular university in providing explicit instruction in the teachings of the faith, teachings that, as I have suggested, themselves derive from the story. Biblical and theological education, along with applications to life embodied in ethical instruction, are indeed central aspects of Christian education. In their commitment to the Christian narrative, Christians agree with Newman that theology is a source of genuine insight and religion should not merely be an object of study. However, this is again not sufficient, in my view. What is needed for Christian education is not simply theological and Biblical education, but an attempt to show how Christian understanding relates to the whole of life. Theological education, important as it is, that is isolated from the main body of human learning cannot do the job.

A natural suggestion at this point is that what must be added to theological education is a focus on the interdisciplinary connections between fields. Christians should not study theology in isolation, but should attempt to think about the nature of God and God's salvation history in relation to all of their thinking and knowing. We are now very close to the right answer on my view. The power of Christian education is indeed closely linked to its ability to help those who are educated see life in a holistic way. Merely thinking of a Christian education as one that includes theology along with an emphasis on interdisciplinary connections is still not quite on target, however.

Interdisciplinary thinking still thinks of Christian education in terms of relating one discipline to another. We need to relate theology and Biblical studies to philosophy, to the arts, and to the natural and social sciences. And this is indeed something that is needed. However, this picture fails to see that what must be related are not simply the various academic disciplines. Rather, the task for each Christian and for the community as a whole is to relate what they do as scholars and teachers to their primary faith-commitments. This is not merely relating one's academic discipline to theology, conceived as another academic discipline, but thinking through the implications of one's own Christian calling to the whole of one's life. And this in turn means seeing what one does as a teacher and a scholar in relation to the primary Christian story that provides the ultimate reference point for all Christian thinking. It is true that theology and its formal study have a special place in articulating that story and engendering an understanding of it. Theologians, however, like other Christian scholars, also must face the task of understanding themselves and their callings in relation to their commitment to Christ. They too must seek to understand what they do as scholars in light of faithfulness to Christ. They too must guard against the temptation to see their scholarly work purely in professional terms. It is quite possible to engage in the academic study of theology without seeing that scholarly effort as service to Christ or his church. Theologians and Biblical scholars, like other Christian scholars, are faced with the challenge to integrate their scholarly lives with their faith.

What would it mean in concrete terms to work as scholars and teachers in relation to a commitment to Christ that is understood against the backdrop of the defining Christian narrative? The answers are of course different for every discipline and perhaps for every issue, and in any case a detailed answer cannot be provided within this paper. Still, it is important to see the range of ways this question can be answered. In some disciplines, most of what Christian scholars learn and teach may be indistinguishable from what their secular colleagues learn and teach, at least with respect to most questions. In my view this is largely the case for the natural sciences and for technical knowledge. A commitment to the basic Christian narrative does not change the chemical composition of an element. But the difference between the sciences and the other disciplines is a matter of degree. What is true for most questions in natural science is true for some questions in every discipline. A formal logical fallacy in philosophy does not become a valid argument because it is put forward by a Christian.

The fact that much Christian scholarship may look just like non-Christian scholarship should not blind us to the relevance that the Christian narrative does have for the work of the scholar. For the Christian natural scientist, the beauty, order, and regularity that the natural world displays are manifestations of the beauty, intelligence, and goodness of the creator. The disorder and suffering that are seen manifest the distortions characteristic of the fall.

The Christian social scientist must see human beings in light of the paradoxical status those humans have in the Biblical narrative—created both as dust of the earth and in the image of God, fallen and yet the object of God's redeeming love. We humans are both solidly part of the natural order and responsible agents who have the power to despoil or enhance that order. We are both fallen creatures who are running away from our own deepest good, and potentially redeemed creatures who are offered union with God and the transformation of human character and relationships. Such a picture of human life may suggest many lines of inquiry as scholars examine human behavior, and many discoveries of the social sciences may take on a different configuration or coloring when held up against the backdrop of such a picture of human life.

The Christian who studies the arts or who creates art must be alive to the spiritual meaning of human existence and the way that meaning is expressed. The philosopher and literary critic do not have to limit themselves to formal questions but can also pay attention to the human quest for significance. Christian engineers must not limit their focus to purely technical questions but must address the proper uses of technology for human flourishing, just as the Christian lawyer must think about the relation between the law and the fundamental justice that the law is supposed to serve. The professor of business must think not only of profit but of the purposes of economic activity and its relation to other human ends. There are thus many scholarly questions that may be suggested by the Biblical narrative or which take different form when framed against the backdrop of that narrative.

Perhaps the most important contribution, however, is made by the fact that the Christian narrative is a common possession of Christian scholars, and thus it provides a narrative framework for understanding how the various fields of human knowledge can and should be connected. As I noted earlier, Newman saw the fields of human knowledge as forming a natural unity, a unity sadly lacking in most contemporary universities. A Christian university should be different for two reasons. First of all, the common story that the community shares provides a basis for what we might call a genuine intellectual community, one that extends even beyond classroom teachers to those who serve the students and campus community in other ways. This common narrative is particularly valuable for the teaching faculty. Even though many faculty work in highly specialized and technical fields, the common Christian commitment provides a basis for genuine intellectual discussion. We may be asking different questions, but as the backdrop for those questions we share a narrative framework that makes university-wide discussion a real possibility.

And this discussion is not limited to discussion of theological and "religious" questions. We all have an interest in seeing how our particular scholarly questions can be related to that story, and as we see this happen, we can at the same time see how questions in one field are related to questions in others. Christian historians may not have a great understanding of sub-atomic particles or even great interest in some of the questions that physicists ask about them, but they should be very interested in how physicists think about the nature of the physical world understood as God's creation. Physicists may not know much about some areas of history, but Christian physicists surely have an interest in how history can be understood as the arena for God's providential ordering of the world. As faculty members relate their disciplines to their common Christian narrative, they simultaneously relate them to all the other disciplines which are being related to that narrative.

Newman's ideal of the university as a place where knowledge, understood as a connected whole, is created and passed down is realized in the Christian university. It is true that the Christian university on my account is only one form of the university, and that there are rivals, some of whom may see the Christian university as inferior. But those who are convinced in faith that the Christian narrative is true should see this narrative as one that enhances and stimulates fruitful inquiry. They should have the courage to stride boldly forward as scholars, confident that the God who is the source of all truth, and the Christ in whom are hid all the treasures of wisdom and knowledge, will bless and sustain their honest and humble efforts.

Notes

[1] John Henry Newman, *The Idea of a University* (Oxford: Oxford University Press, 1976) 5. I have removed the emphases in Newman's original.

[2] Newman 5.

[3] George Marsden, "The Soul of the American University," *The Secularization of the Academy*, ed. George M. Marsden and Bradley J. Longfield (New York: Oxford University Press, 1992) 11.

[4] Quoted in Bradley J. Longfield, "From Evangelicalism to Liberalism," *The Secularization of the Academy* 56.

[5] One should note that here and elsewhere the term "public university" is being used in its American sense to refer to universities such as our great state universities. The term should not be confused with the English usage in which a "public school" is a private institution, often a boarding school. However, a good case can be made that many private universities, such as Stanford and the Ivy League schools, are "public" in the sense that they intend to serve the public good and strive to embody the same ideals as the state universities. I do not therefore necessarily equate "public" with "state-funded." In any case, the rise in philanthropy among state schools, and the growth of government support for research in private schools has narrowed the distinction between private and state university.

[6] Newman 50.

[7] Newman 71. I read Newman's reference here to "public schools" as referring not solely to private high schools such as Eton but to institutions of higher learning in general that serve the public good, including universities such as Oxford and Cambridge. Otherwise, his claims here would have little relevance to his argument about the university.

[8] Newman 73-74.

[9] See Newman 43. Newman here discusses the attempt to view religion as related to "feelings" and "poetry." This is part of the reason Newman feels the need for a Catholic university, which would uphold the intellectual viability of theology.

[10] Richard Hughes, *How Christian Faith Can Sustain the Life of the Mind* (Grand Rapids: Wm. B. Eerdmans, 2001) 11. See especially Chapter 4, "The

Power of the Christian Traditions," where I take it that the use of the plural is significant.

[11] Richard Hughes, *Models for Christian Higher Education* (Grand Rapids: Wm. B. Eerdmans, 1997).

[12] *Models* 5.

[13] *Models* 6.

[14] *Models* 7.

[15] Some would prefer to divide the fourth act and distinguish between salvation and sanctification, but I prefer to keep these closely linked.

[16] See James McLendon, *Systematic Theology: Ethics* Vol. 1 (Nashville: Abingdon, 1986) 143.

Chapter 3

The Christian Narrative and Secular Academia

James Bennighof

Stephen Evans contends that the essence of the Christian university implies that scholars within such a community "are faced with the challenge to integrate their scholarly lives with their faith." In order to clarify the components of this faith, Evans sets forth a basic narrative which he says constitutes part of the common heritage of the Christian tradition, a heritage defined and elaborated by scripture.

Evans argues for the validity of the Christian university, among other universities, conceding that other types of universities also have their place in our educational system. Beyond this assumption of coexistence, he does not explore how the Christian university and other universities might relate to one another, or how ideas or conclusions reached in the respective institutions might be related.

In my response, I wish to focus on the latter issue. If a university attempts to be a Christian university as Evans defines it, on the scale that Baylor intends in the 2012 vision, how will the ideas that it propagates relate to those cultivated at other institutions? I would like to suggest that, while all these institutions may coexist, if the Christian university truly seeks to integrate this narrative with its scholarly life, there may be some ways in which they will not coexist comfortably. In particular, I think that this integration will lead to some conclusions at the Christian institution that are irreconcilable with generally accepted notions in secular academia, with the natural implication that one line of reasoning must be seen as superior to the other. As I will explain at the end of this paper, while this irreconcilability may bring obvious negative consequences in the form of antagonism from scholars in the secular realm, it also, and more crucially, may bring positive consequences as a result of the unique insights that the Christian narrative yields.

The irreconcilability between the two perspectives may not appear within some disciplines, especially within certain boundaries of technical exploration. Evans has addressed this issue, noting that "a commitment to the basic Christian narrative does not change the chemical composition of an element." Such technical questions occupy a greater proportion of scholarly attention in some disciplines than in others—perhaps more in mathematics, for example, and less in ethics. Evans says, however, that scholars in all fields are obligated to look beyond these purely technical questions. When they do, it seems to me, scholars committed to this integration of the narrative with the scholarly life can reach conclusions that differ radically from those reached by others who do not share those commitments.

I shall mention briefly two fairly simple examples from the social sciences. Does the Christian clinical psychologist consider it to be essential to his understanding of human behavior that sin exists and that, without the redeeming work of Christ, no person can be truly free from guilt? If he does, he may disagree with much of the profession, and his position would probably influence his assessment of therapeutic strategies in ways that others might find absurd.

In anthropology or sociology, is it relevant for the scholar to compare the accepted practices of a culture with those established by God and to find some cultures inferior to others on that basis? I suspect that few anthropology or sociology textbooks would hint at the desirability of making any such value judgment, let alone one based on the Christian narrative.

Let me comment at slightly greater length within my own realm, that of criticism in the humanities. When literary scholars examine a work of fiction, it is quite common for them to find questions of integrity relevant, even if this is sometimes only tacitly the case. Integrity can take many different forms, from a simple matter of coherence within the text, to a sense of artistic and personal honesty on the part of the author. It can be a conclusion that revelations within the text about all manner of things—human relationships, social justice, aesthetic value, perhaps—are consistent with the way of the world. A lack of integrity in one or more of these areas will often have implications for a critic's measure of the quality of the work, rendering verdicts on the work such as "incoherent," "cynical," and "facile," even if the issues of integrity are not explicitly set forth.

In this sort of critical undertaking, suppose that a novel portrays a protagonist as having finally reached a state of reconciliation with the world around him, with no reference to any engagement with the redeeming work of Christ. Is it appropriate for the Christian scholar to conclude that the novel is perhaps sincere and consistent with the worldviews of many people, but ultimately naïve with respect to cosmic reality? In my view, the Christian narrative suggests that such a conclusion would indeed be appropriate and, in fact, would reflect a crucial insight not otherwise possible. However, I have my doubts about whether an article featuring this perspective would be well-received by a top-tier literary journal with an editorial board made up of those who do not subscribe to the same narrative.

A central issue that comes into play in all these examples is the status that we accord to propositions that proceed from our faith commitment. Do we consider these to have equal weight with others? For example, do we consider the propositions that Christ was born of a virgin, that he was God incarnate, that he died and in three days was resurrected to be historical facts on a par with the assassination of Lincoln or the fall of the Roman empire, even though some of the former may not be demonstrable in the same way that some of the latter are? If not, in what sense can we say that we truly believe the former?

I have suggested some ways that faith-informed scholarship may vary from scholarship that does not integrate the faith narrative into its set of assumptions. The way that scholarly conversations about these matters might actually play out is more complex than I have implied, but I have highlighted just a few issues simply to make the point that a genuine incorporation of the faith-based narrative into the content of our scholarly lives will probably be rather jarringly inconsistent with the assumptions of many disciplines. If this is true, it should not surprise us, based on our knowledge of the narrative itself, that those who reject the narrative, including the secular scholarly community, are likely to be antagonistic towards it.

There are reasons to shy away from the whole-hearted commitment to this integration of the Christian narrative that Evans has outlined. The results of such a plan would surely fly in the face of currently received academic thought, and thus we might suffer misunderstanding and often risk being accused of anti-intellectualism without grounds for such an accusation.

However, in spite of these risks, I think there are powerful reasons to boldly seize this initiative. Put negatively, to do anything less would confine our commitment to this narrative to some private realm not susceptible to scrutiny by others. Even more, though, if we do integrate the Christian narrative decisively and visibly into our scholarly work, it will have a liberating effect. While others might imagine that adherence to this narrative would limit our inquiry, I argue that these kinds of limitations—that is, the ruling out or depreciation of some options—will actually free our scholarship, because it will only rule out what we believe to be false. And, in turn, as our scholarship is transformed, we may have the tremendous privilege of participating in redemptive acts, as those to whom our scholarship is communicated become aware of the ways that our faith narrative influences our interpretation of our world and transforms our lives.

Chapter 4

The Sciences at a Christian University

Marianna A. Busch

Let me begin by saying how delighted I am to have been invited to participate in this event. It gives me a very public opportunity to thank Don Schmeltekopf for his years of service as provost and to acknowledge the contributions he has made to Baylor. All department chairs have worked closely with him over the past twelve years, but I was fortunate also to be involved in a very special project that he spearheaded—establishment of the Baylor BIC program. Prior to setting up this program, Don Schmeltekopf, Bob Baird, Bill Cooper, Wallace Daniel, Ben Pierce, and I journeyed to Asheville, North Carolina, to attend a conference on general education. At this conference I learned first-hand the depth of Don's commitment to undergraduate education and his desire to foster interdisciplinary studies. This was an experience that has colored my thinking about both undergraduate and graduate education through the years that have followed.

I also consider it a privilege to be here, first, because I am Lutheran, not Baptist, and, second, because my discipline, chemistry, lies near the left of Evans "relevance continuum."[1] This continuum runs from mathematics and natural science on the left to theology on the right. Presumably, the closer the discipline lies toward theology, the greater the impact that Christian faith has on questions in that discipline. As Baylor 2012 was being formulated, I was rather distressed to hear that some might interpret this position on the continuum to mean that the natural sciences had only a modest claim to importance in a Christian university.

I want to make it clear that I am a practitioner of science. I am not trained in philosophy and certainly not in theology. That said, it seems to me, as a scientist, very foolish to suppose that science could ever "prove" the existence of God or demonstrate beyond doubt that the universe was created by the hand of God. I know all too well that science is a very human endeavor.[2] It is a human attempt to observe and understand the natural world. Given our human limitations, we can only "see through a glass darkly." When dealing with the unknown, we may extrapolate or interpolate, but neither of these is adequate to deal with the new and unexpected. Openness to the implications of the experimental "outlier" and to new ideas makes for really good science. Scientific surprises have produced such revolutions as quantum theory, the big bang theory, and modern genetics, to name a few.[3]

As a practicing scientist, I also believe that scientific principles can never replace man's need for religion and an understanding of the meaning of life. For example, logic has been used to argue that it is better to believe than not to believe. If the believer is correct, he gains a great reward. If he is not correct, he loses nothing. The non-believer, however, runs a great risk. If he is right, he loses nothing. If he is wrong, he inherits eternal damnation. Thus, the argument goes, it is better to believe than not to believe. But such logic is cold comfort when dealing with life's many problems. As a Lutheran, I also know we are saved by grace through faith. "If it is the adherents of the law who are to be the heirs, faith is null and the promise is void."[4]

The 1960s film *The Seventh Seal*, by the Swedish director Ingmar Bergman, is set in Europe in the 1300s, during the second pandemic of the Black Death. The two major characters in this film contrast the approach of faith and intellect in dealing with the eternal question, "Is there a God?" The knight, an intellectual, continuously searches for proof of God's existence, consulting learned men, a young girl accused of witchcraft, and finally Death itself, but he never finds a satisfactory answer. By contrast, the simple man of faith sees proof of God's existence everywhere. Though we cannot find satisfactory answers to these fundamental religious questions through science, our faith connects God to what we understand by reason alone. By hiring men and women of faith, in the ecumenical Christian sense, I believe Baylor can demonstrate that, for many faculty, recognizing the connectedness of knowledge becomes almost second nature. Thus, careful hiring practices are central to achieving Baylor 2012 and are appropriately treated in a separate paper in this symposium.[5]

Construction of the new 500,000 square foot science building is clear evidence of Baylor's commitment to the natural sciences. Baylor 2012 also points out the relevance of science to Christian stewardship of the environment and human health.[6] Nevertheless, and I hope I am wrong, I continue to be concerned with what I perceive as a lingering uneasiness about the role at Baylor of disciplines on the far left of Evans' spectrum, the physical sciences in particular. With our 2012 emphasis focused on medicine and the environment, have we fully demonstrated the connectedness of all knowledge in science? What is this connectedness and what role might the physical sciences play at Baylor?

This year marks the 50th anniversary of the elucidation of the structure of DNA, so it is perhaps appropriate to use DNA to illustrate how connected the scientific enterprise can be.[7] An understanding of the structure of DNA, which is arguably the most important of all molecules to our understanding of life and human health, required the knowledge and intuition of a geneticist and a biophysicist, data obtained using instrumentation developed by a physicist, and molecular modeling and chemical bonding concepts developed by chemists. The scientific disciplines are a very connected branch of knowledge and the solution to important scientific problems almost always requires an interdisciplinary approach.

Aside from supporting Baylor's emphasis on human health and the environment, what other role might the physical sciences play? I have attended two lectures this past week, both given by Nobel Laureates, Prof. Alan MacDiarmid[8] and Prof. Richard Smalley.[9] Each spoke urgently about the need for American science to pay increased attention to the physical sciences. While America leads the world in biotechnology and computer technology, and is likely to continue to do so for many years, we are falling behind in the physical sciences. Asian citizens now earn approximately five times more Ph.D. degrees in physical science and engineering than U.S. citizens, and most are now earning these degrees in some very fine Asian institutions. While the number of degrees granted to Asian citizens continues to climb rapidly, the number of degrees granted to U.S. citizens is gradually declining. If these trends continue, by 2010 over 90% of all physical scientists and engineers in the world will be Asians working in Asia.[10] Such a situation would seriously erode our ability to compete and to develop very important new technologies that depend on the physical sciences.

Humanity's top ten problems for the next fifty years are most likely to include all or most of the following:

(1) energy	(6) terrorism and war
(2) water	(7) disease
(3) food	(8) education
(4) the environment	(9) threats to democracy
(5) poverty	(10) population.[11]

It can be easily argued that developing cheap, carbon-free, safe sources of energy would have a major impact on solving at least five other problems on this list, i.e., water, food, the environment, poverty, and war.

Sometime over the next decade, or perhaps two decades, our production of oil is predicted to peak, while the world's need for energy will double, triple, and by 2050 perhaps even quadruple, depending on population increases and energy demands from developing nations such as China and India. This makes clean, cheap energy the single most important problem facing humanity today. Solutions to the energy problem will be found primarily by physical scientists and engineers. This country has an urgent need for more citizens trained in the physical sciences. I believe Christian stewardship of the environment, human health, and the welfare of society in general also dictate that we address the energy issue and give proper support to all the sciences, including the physical sciences. While it is true that Baylor cannot afford to support everything, there are some things we simply must not fail to support.

Notes

---

[1] Stephen Evans, "Christian Scholarship and the Biblical Drama," quoted in "The Implications of the Baptist and Christian Character of Baylor University for Hiring, Tenure, and Promotion: The Significant Contribution Model," Mikeal Parsons, Colloquy, paper no. 2, 10 Apr. 2003.

[2] Del Ratzsch, *Science and Its Limits* (InterVarsity Press: Leichester, England) 92-99.

[3] See Pete Moore, *E=mc²: The Great Ideas that Shaped Our World* (Friedman/Fairfax Publishers, 2002).

[4] Rom. 4:14.

[5] "The Implications of the Baptist and Christian Character of Baylor University for Hiring, Tenure, and Promotion: The Significant Contribution Model," Mikeal Parsons, Colloquy, paper no. 2, 10 Apr. 2003.

[6] Baylor 2012: Ten Year Vision, 5.

[7] See James D. Watson, *The Double Helix: A Personal Account of the Discovery of the Structure of DNA* (Simon & Schuster: New York, 1968).

[8] Alan G. MacDiarmid. "Science, People and Energy: What Does the Future Hold?" Gooch-Stephens Lecture. Baylor University. Waco, TX. April 3, 2002.

[9] Richard Smalley, "Nanotechnology for Energy Prosperity." Council for Chemical Research. Austin, TX. April 8, 2002. <http://www.ruf.rice.edu/~smalleyg/Presentations/PCAST%20March%203,%202003.ppt. Used with permission.

[10] Smalley.

[11] Smalley.

Chapter 5

University or Multiversity?

Gerald B. Cleaver

My response to Stephen Evans' paper is entitled *University or Multiversity?* It is inspired by the recent Templeton Foundation cosmology conference, *Universe or Multiverse?*, held at Stanford University. The conference examined the possibility of the existence of other universes physically disconnected from our own both in space and in time. Such universes are predicted in chaotic inflation theory, which provides one possible explanation of how God created our universe. In chaotic inflation models, these physically independent universes, sometimes termed microverses, can possess vastly differing physical laws.

The destiny of many institutions of higher education today is to become distributed collections of programs lacking the cohesiveness of a common understanding or perspective. As the independent universes have no unifying physical laws, these institutions often have no underlying, consistent world-view. Thus the title of my talk results from the analogy I see between the typical center of higher learning, which I will call a multiversity, and the multiverse concept. Both are composed of numerous (albeit perhaps infinite for the latter) separate components and lack a global unifying factor.

In a collegiate *multi*versity, method is often separated from meaning, and process is independent of purpose. Within a given *multi*versity what is perceived as truth varies between schools. The lack of a coherent world-view within a multiversity is perhaps exemplified by a state college I visited a few years ago that supported, along with first-tier science departments, a journalism department that, in all seriousness, included an astrology section in its campus newspaper. Even truth and reality can appear "essentially contested" within a multiversity.

According to Evans, such an institution of higher learning lacks a necessary element to qualify as a "university in the fullest sense of the word." I emphatically agree. A true *uni*versity places the entirety of its activities within an enveloping *Weltanschauung*, a world-view connecting all knowledge taught within. A university instills a philosophy of life, nature, and history. It re-unites meaning to methods, purpose to processes.

As an institution of higher education, Baylor possesses the three essential and inter-connected elements of a *uni*versity in the fullest sense of the word: its Christian foundation empowers and shapes its pursuit of continuing excellence in both teaching and research. Further, no deeper or more self-consistent world-view could be held by a university than one formulated on foundational Christian tenets and realized by the "grand drama" of faithful lives serving the campus community and beyond. Therein, faculty are encouraged to pursue whatever is true, honorable, right, pure, lovely, good, excellent, and praise-worthy because of their common belief that the author and finisher of these is Himself truth. Thus, Baylor's programs in any of the general academic disciplines mentioned in the 2012 report: logic and mathematics, conceptual analysis, literary criticism, historiography, and the various methodologies of the sciences, become fulfillments of Paul's Philippians 4:8: "Finally, brothers, whatever is true, whatever is noble, whatever is right, whatever is pure, whatever is lovely, whatever is admirable—if anything is excellent or praiseworthy—think about such things."

While the schools within a *multi*versity or a *uni*versity both facilitate the discovery of new knowledge, at a university "under the cross" this pursuit is intended for the glory of God and the betterment of humanity.

Having spoken of *uni*versities and *multi*versities in most general terms, I will now direct my comments toward my own research fields of elementary particles, string theory, and early universe cosmology. I want to mention how liberating and personally fulfilling I have found research and teaching at Baylor. At few other *uni*versities, and at still fewer *multi*versities, would it have been possible both to continue research in string theory and to develop a science and theology course from the Christian perspective. Baylor is one of those rare universities where the unity is understood between studying the physics of the universe an infinitesimal fraction of a second after its creation 13.7 billion years ago, and teaching a course on the transcendence and immanence of God and the related means by which His divine will is realized in the universe. In contrast, a typical multiversity would allow the research but generally prohibit the course, while the insular sectarian colleges discussed in the 2012 report would prohibit the research, but allow the course (albeit likely under constraints).

By rejecting the false division "between the uncompromised pursuit of intellectual excellence and intense faithfulness to the Christian tradition" and instead holding the view that the "highest intellectual excellence is fully compatible with orthodox Christian devotion," that science and faith are "not only compatible but mutually reinforcing,"[1] Baylor truly can "profoundly affect the world . . . emerging as one of the world's leading universities."[2] For example, the elementary particle physics faculty at Baylor will soon include two leading members of research teams at Fermilab and CERN, the two premiere particle physics centers in the world. Baylor's string cosmology group will also soon welcome a general relativist exploring M-theory applications and/or a cosmologist examining the cosmic microwave background, likewise cutting-edge research fields. These groups at Baylor have the potential to become a national powerhouse, providing another example of the fruit of Baylor's undivided path.

Einstein once opined that the most incomprehensible thing about the universe is that it is comprehensible. Through the scientific pursuits, the physical truths of this universe are being understood at levels unimaginable only a century, and sometimes even just decades, ago. These truths are, however, associated primarily with "how" questions. Neither for Einstein, nor for us, do physical truths answer the "why" questions. This is, I believe, the issue at the crux of Einstein' thoughts. By its nature, a *multi*versity cannot provide an adequate answer to Einstein's enigma since it is based not upon a genuine all-inclusive *Weltanschauung* but upon several competing ones at best. Instead, resolution is left to the universities, especially the universities "under the cross," where the legitimacy of both discovered knowledge, which answers the how questions, and revealed knowledge, which answers the why questions, is affirmed. The Christian university's world-view professes that in creating and preserving the universe, God has endowed it with contingent order and intelligibility, providing the basis for scientific investigation.[3] In essence, scientific discovery is understood as continually revealing the blueprints of God's creation in ever finer detail.

I would like to consider now the methods by which discovered knowledge from the physical universe and revealed knowledge from scripture are obtained, since the Christian university's *Weltanschauung* develops from both arenas. Robert B. Fischer, former Provost of Biola University, Professor Emeritus of Chemistry, and former Dean of the School of Sciences, California State University, argues that the two processes are, in fact, parallel in several respects. Fischer claims that,

> . . . in each process there is (a) input, which consists essentially of "what there is" in the Bible or in the realm of nature, but this is only the beginning of the process. The observational input leads to (b) interpretation and other processing of that input by appropriate methodology, which leads to (c) output, commonly designated biblical or theological explanation or as scientific explanation. The output leads to (d) prediction of further observational tests and test results to prove or to negate that explanation and thus to a repetition of the cycle.[4]

He further emphasizes that

> The methodologies of interpretation used in step (b) with the two sources of information are essentially similar in principle but different in some practical ways because of the different sources of input. The term "rational inquiry" is applicable to both. Indeed, the overall processes of gaining information from the Bible and from the scientific investigation of nature are so similar that is was fashionable in an earlier era to refer to theology as the queen of the sciences—"sciences" because of the methodology and "queen" because its subject matter deals with a transcendent God.[5]

For Christians, both sources of knowledge should be taken as authoritative. In prior ages, these were viewed as God's general and special revelations. Importantly, though, study of scripture and study of nature both require interpretation. This is necessary in biblical study because of language, context, history, and culture issues, for the meaning and the reality are in the interpretation, not just in the words. Interpretation is also necessary in study of the natural world. First, there are limitations to the accuracy of human observations of the physical world, either through direct use of the senses or through use of observational and measuring devices. Second, interpretation of a scientific explanation or equation itself is required by anyone seeking to understand it. Third, an outcome of an experiment can be multi-determined. That is, more than one theory may provide explanation for a given set of data. Fourth, the validity of a theory is never absolutely proven. Rather, the possibility always exists that future experiments may prove a theory invalid in certain limits. For example, Newtonian mechanics was found to be invalid as velocities approach the speed of light and became only an approximation of Einstein's relativity in the low velocity limit. Today, both relativity and quantum mechanics are being replaced by string theory in the highest energy limit.

Fischer acknowledges that methodological differences do exist, of course, between theological and scientific studies. In particular, the subject matters should be properly limited to that which is contained in the respective sources. Each discipline deals with some types of subject matter on which the other is silent. Fischer stresses, however, that there can be other areas of subject matter in which both studies provide knowledge. A Christian university "in the largest sense of the word" is particularly suited to investigate these areas of overlap. Here it can play a unique role since neither the fork of the path chosen by *multi*versities nor the insulated path followed by some religious colleges offers a sufficient world-view to meet this challenge.

While the processes for obtaining theological and scientific knowledge have similarities, Fischer stresses that to traverse the undivided path, a university should regard equally the two types of knowledge while strongly distinguishing between their differing roles and character. Otherwise, a path diverges towards what he calls "scientism" if a tendency develops wherein knowledge of the natural sciences is applied beyond its appropriate domain, or else the path bends towards "biblicism" wherein biblical knowledge is seen as valid but purely scientific knowledge is not. For Fischer, the effect of limiting one's confident knowledge to that obtained either from scientific investigation alone or from the Bible alone is to limit God unduly, for the same God is responsible for both.[6]

Beyond equal recognition, theological knowledge and scientific knowledge must not be treated as in opposition, but rather as complementary. Answers to who and why questions and answers to how questions are found on different planes. False dichotomies, such as the (in)famous "God versus chance/natural processes," have diverted the paths of many institutions of higher learning towards either scientism or biblicism. The unified path remains possible for a Christian university when there is distinction between God, as the source of all creation, and natural processes, as His usual chosen creative method. For the Christian world-view of the unified path, the God of scripture is the primary fact, the originator and sustainer of the realms of nature and of faith. God is the unifying factor from which all else derives existence and meaning.

Most institutions of higher education have not been able to follow a unified path. Many have broken from the path altogether, becoming *multi*versities lacking a unifying world-view. Others have remained as *uni*versities, possessing an overall world-view, but having chosen the diverging paths of either scientism or biblicism. There are, thankfully, a few remaining *uni*versities traveling the unified path of the Christian *Weltanschauung*. Baylor is indeed one of these. The ten-year vision, to which much is owed Provost Schmeltekopf, will vastly extend and strengthen Baylor's travels along this path. I am excited to be a member of the community sharing in this experience and journey.

Notes

[1] Baylor 2012: Ten-Year Vision, 8.
[2] Baylor 2012: Ten-Year Vision, 12.
[3] Doctrinal Statement of Faith of the American Scientific Affiliation.
[4] Fischer, Robert B., *God Did It, But How? Relationships Between the Bible and Science* (Ipswich: ASA Press, 1997) 8.
[5] Fischer 8.
[6] Fischer 92-95.

Chapter 6

The Integration of Faith and Scientific Inquiry

M. David Rudd

As a psychologist or, perhaps even more appropriately, as a clinical and/or social scientist, I would like to add a somewhat different voice to the discussion. In addition, perhaps my limited tenure at Baylor—only four years—also provides a unique perspective, but more about that later.

From an organizational standpoint, I will arrange my comments around several themes identified in Stephen Evans' manuscript. I think I would be remiss, though, if I didn't couch my comments within the broader debate on and off campus about Baylor 2012. Additionally, I will attempt to follow the commonly accepted *law of parsimony*, something I'm sure will be appreciated, perhaps even enthusiastically encouraged. Accordingly, I will not repeat issues verbatim, but summarize where appropriate, making the most of the time and space allotted for a response.

Evans makes a well-defined and compelling case for the Christian university, as an ideal and a reality. Let me summarize. First, Evans argues that a Christian university makes a special and valuable contribution to the contemporary higher education community, a contribution that is not isolated, but fits within the broader national and international community of universities. It is important to view Baylor within this context. Second, despite theological distinctives, Christian denominations share common and identifiable beliefs. Third, the Christian university is defined as a community of individuals committed to these core beliefs and the *basic Christian story*. Fourth, these Christian beliefs have relevance to the academic mission, that is, the development and transmission of knowledge. And finally, all knowledge and learning are interconnected and, *if God is taken out of the equation*, the net result is intellectual incoherence and fragmentation. Christian beliefs can inform scholarship in meaningful and important ways, regardless of discipline or subspecialty.

Of the above points, I would hazard to say that most Baylor faculty members, perhaps a considerable majority, would agree with the first three. It is the fourth that draws the sharpest disagreement, particularly from those in the sciences and social sciences. Moreover, this is a central point of criticism against Baylor 2012 and Baylor's aspiration to achieve excellence in scholarship. So, if we agree on more than we disagree, why the intensity and duration of debate? First, it may well be the academic tradition; we are (and I proudly include myself in this group) trained to argue and prove points. Second, as has been noted elsewhere, contemporary research universities are characterized by overspecialization and fragmentation of academic disciplines, a fact often cited as a major reason that tier-one aspirations may be inappropriate for Baylor. Though Evans has made a case for the *connectedness of knowledge*, that argument needs to be explored, not just philosophically, but empirically. In short, as a clinical scientist, I say, "Show me the data." Let us not suspend empirical evidence in favor of emotionally laden arguments. Rather, at the point of greatest importance, let us make sure we employ the scientific method in our scientific inquiry.

To some degree, this reluctance to agree that the "connectedness of knowledge" has been demonstrated has been a factor in the debate about Baylor 2012, at least from my perspective. I've heard on more than a few occasions that faith simply cannot inform scientific inquiry. The vast majority of us were trained in traditional institutions that favored intellectual and practical fragmentation; thus, for most, if not all of us, Baylor 2012 requires us to venture into a new arena. This can be invigorating or frightening, depending on personal history, interpretation, or understanding of this new arena, and the perceived consequences of entering it.

Let us consider how some of the data in psychology and neuroscience might answer the question of whether or not faith can inform scientific inquiry. The National Institutes of Health currently funds substantial projects at some of the nation's most prestigious universities, including Duke, Pennsylvania, Georgetown, Miami, and Dartmouth, all targeting prayer and personal faith in some fashion.

Many of these studies are randomized clinical trials, documenting the effectiveness of prayer and faith in maintaining health, in recovering from illness or surgery, and in addressing overall well being, happiness, and healthy emotional functioning. One of these studies actually explores variability in functional imaging of the brain for those who pray as opposed to those who don't, in essence looking at the neuroscientific basis of prayer. Duke maintains perhaps the most prominent center in this area, the Center for the Study of Religion, Spirituality, and Health. Why should we not have such a center at Baylor?

When we look at the data, it is clear that faith can inform scientific inquiry. It may not always be obvious, but there are nevertheless identifiable connections, consistent with the notion of the *connectedness of knowledge*. Does this mean that this is all that Baylor should do? Absolutely not. The full spectrum of activities is critical, something readily identified and acknowledged in Evans' paper. In fact, from a more personal perspective and speaking as a psychologist, I'm not quite sure how any psychologist could separate values, beliefs, and core convictions from what that same psychologist does in clinical practice.

Another issue that has surfaced in response to Baylor 2012 is the fear that Baylor will sacrifice its identity as a traditionally well-respected teaching university on the altar of research. Dean Wallace Daniel's recent column in the *Waco Tribune-Herald* addresses some of the misconceptions inherent in this assumption, providing evidence that recent hires have admirably served, not just the research mission of the university, but its teaching mission as well. The anti-research argument in particular highlights a too common problem: in the absence of solid empirical data, we frequently see what we're looking for and cling to that with which we're most familiar.

There are numerous assumptions embedded in the argument that Baylor will sacrifice its distinctiveness as a teaching university in its pursuit of tier-one status and in its concerted effort to strengthen its Christian identity. First is the assumption that good researchers can not be good teachers, or, if they could be good teachers, they won't be able to give adequate time to their teaching responsibilities to become good teachers. Second is the notion that the only reason that Baylor achieved a reputation as an exceptional teaching institution is that it did not require faculty members to demonstrate scholarship in order to achieve tenure. At times I have referred to this as the *Lake Woebegone hypothesis*, that Baylor was a place where all the teachers

were exceptional and all the students eager to learn.   Like any
community, Baylor reflects diversity and always has. There have been
many exceptional teachers here, and there have been average teachers
here. In any case, Baylor has always been in the knowledge and
scholarship business. As former University of Texas President Peter
Flawn has said, "universities are in the knowledge business,
generating it, transmitting it, and disseminating it." Rather than argue
this issue as a matter of opinion and emotion, let us look at the facts.
Recent revisions in tenure and promotion criteria require exceptional
teaching. As we think about tenure and promotion, let us remember,
as Peter Flawn has noted, "Tenure should not be awarded for
satisfactory, adequate, or good performance. It should be awarded
only in recognition of superior performance."

Can Baylor 2012 be achieved?   Yes. Will it be easy? No. As I
read Baylor 2012 and reflect on the aspiration for tier-one status, I
personally view it as a call to excellence. This is a unique opportunity,
a chance to establish a vital academic community founded, nurtured,
and maintained in Christian values. What attracted me to Baylor? The
opportunity to participate in this grand experiment.   As a clinical
psychologist and scientist, I rely on my Christian faith as well as the
foundations of my training. The data I see at present are compelling.
Baylor has an exceptional opportunity simultaneously to strengthen
its Christian character and to achieve excellence in scholarship. Are
there risks? Certainly. Is it worth the effort? Absolutely. Will it spark
vigorous debate? I certainly hope so.

Part Two

*Implications of Christian Identity for
Faculty Hiring, Tenure, and Promotion*

Chapter 7

Building the Faculty at a Christian University: The Significant Contribution Model

Mikeal C. Parsons

Introduction

First, let me acknowledge what is surely apparent to anyone who knows me. I hold no distinct place at Baylor University from which to claim special knowledge about the implications for the Baptist and Christian character of Baylor for hiring, tenure, and promotion. I have never published in the field of Christian higher education, as several of you have, nor have I held an administrative post of any significance at the university, which might afford special insight into these issues. Thus, none of my remarks should be taken as necessarily representative of the current administration's thoughts or policies.

Nevertheless, I stand here as a relatively long-time faculty member who believes the most recent version of this original vision, the Baylor 2012 vision statement, with its ambitious and far-reaching twin goals of increasing academic excellence and enhancing an already-robust commitment to the Christian tradition, to be the most exciting development on the campus in my seventeen years. I enthusiastically affirm both the religious and academic vision I see there, and, I am delighted to be asked to contribute to this colloquy, which honors the administrative, intellectual, and indeed spiritual legacy of Donald Schmeltekopf.[1]

The Baptist and Christian Character of Baylor University

In order to understand the implications of Baylor's religious character on policies and practices surrounding hiring, tenure, and promotion at Baylor, it would seem appropriate first to take up the question of what is meant by what the program calls the "Baptist and Christian" character. Let me acknowledge from the outset what I detect to be some ambiguity or perhaps even tension between these two descriptors, Baptist and Christian. What is to be the proper relationship between these two adjectives? Are we a Baptist university? Or a Christian university? I would like to put forward the thesis that "Christian" *primarily* addresses the issue of the *substance* of Baylor's religious character and that "Baptist" *primarily* speaks to the *perspective*—the attitudes and practices—with and in which that substance is expressed.[2]

I do not mean to suggest that our Baptist identity has nothing to contribute to the substance of what it means to be a Christian university. Those issues for which Baptists became known, however—believer's baptism by immersion, religious liberty, the priesthood of all believers, the separation of church and state, among others—are, in most cases, practices of or attitudes toward certain issues of faith. Baptist distinctives, by themselves, however, are not enough to sustain the religious commitments of a Christian university. I should hasten to add that I would put most, if not all, other Protestant denominational distinctives—Methodist, Lutheran, etc.—in this same category. The 2012 document reflects a similar distinction of substance and practice when it claims that our goal is "to make Baylor an excellent university whose *foundation* rests on our ecumenical Christian mission, *energized* by our Baptist heritage" (my emphasis).[3]

So I suggest that when we are discussing implications of the *substance* of the religious character of the university on hiring, tenure, and promotion, we should speak and think primarily about the "Christian" character of Baylor, which Baptists have historically affirmed. One reason for this distinction is that many folk use the notion of the "Baptist" university to present a weakened version of the religious dimensions of the university.[4] The argument usually goes something like this: since Baptists have historically stood for religious liberty and tolerance, then as a Baptist university, Baylor should not infuse any particular theological criteria into its faculty appointment process; in other words, the Baptist distinctive of "freedom" would dictate an inclusive policy with regard to religious matters of potential or current faculty members. This kind of argument reminds me of a quip by a literary critic who, in trying to explain the way in which gaps function in the postmodern novel, remarked: "How do you make a doughnut? Start with the hole. How to make a narrative? In the same way."[5]

However appropriate this comment might be for the composition of the contemporary novel, having peered with my two sons through Shipley's window at the bakers on many a Saturday morning, I am skeptical that this is the way to make a good doughnut! I am utterly convinced that this is certainly no way to make a Baptist and Christian university. Emphasizing only one particular interpretation of a selected item of a Baptist distinctive, "freedom," produces a university with a "hole" in its center, a "Krispy Kreme" university, if you will. The predictable path toward secularism of what were originally vital Christian colleges and universities who chose some insipid term such as "tolerance," or "openness," or "freedom" as the defining vocabulary of their mission is well-documented and need not be recounted here.[6]

The Baptist hallmark of religious liberty, of course, has much to contribute to a Christian university. In a now famous quotation, Thomas Helwys, one of the Baptist founders, said, "Let them be heretics, Turks, Jews, or whatsoever, it appertains not the earthly powers to punish them in the least measure."[7] It is entirely appropriate as a matter of practice for this view to shape a response that is warm and welcoming to persons, especially students, of all faiths or no faith at all, a sincere form of Christian hospitality. I doubt seriously, however, anachronisms aside, that Helwys would have imagined using this notion of religious liberty as the defining substantive criterion for faculty tenure at a Baptist university.

Yet this seems to be exactly the path pursued today by some so-called "moderate" Baptists whose self-identity has not moved beyond defining themselves as "anti-fundamentalists" and who wish somehow to preserve the "Baptist" identity of educational institutions.[8] In fact, we find this sentiment, or something very close to it, in the essays prepared recently by Professor Kent Gilbreath in response to the 2012 vision. While the essays focus primarily on strategies for increasing faculty participation in university governance, Gilbreath begins his analysis by assessing the 2012 document itself. Gilbreath claims that "the traditions of 'free will' and the 'priesthood of the believer,' are at the heart of the Baptist faith."[9] Gilbreath further expresses the concern that "Baylor's potential for sliding down the slippery slope toward theological intolerance is one of the greatest

concerns about 'Baylor 2012' to many Baylor faculty members."
Gilbreath attempts to resolve his misgivings about Baylor 2012 by
appeal to principles, exactly the right place to start, in my judgment.

Gilbreath claims to have an "unfocused uneasiness about the general tone of the 'Vision.'"[10] Along the way, Gilbreath draws many
parallels between the "tone" of the 2012 document and the fundamentalists' takeover of the Southern Baptist Convention, which, if true,
would be very chilling, indeed. I trust Gilbreath is not invoking the
term "fundamentalist" as a Shibboleth to stir fear among those for
whom the term evokes memories of the worst kind of religious wars,
but I must confess that, when I read the 2012 document, I am at a loss
to see even "the slightest hint" of a crypto-fundamentalist's agenda.
Consider, for example, these quotations—one from the mission
statement of Criswell College, and the other from the Baylor 2012
statement. From the mission statement of Criswell College:

> The Criswell College exists to provide biblical, theological, professional, and applied education on both the undergraduate and graduate levels, based on an institutional commitment to biblical inerrancy . . . .[11]

Compare this statement with the following from Baylor 2012:

> Because the Church, the one truly democratic and multi-cultural community, is not identical with any denomination, we believe that Baylor will serve best, recruit more effectively, and both preserve and enrich its Baptist identity more profoundly, if we draw our faculty, staff, and students from the full range of Christian traditions.[12]

I cannot imagine any institution with a fundamentalist agenda including this latter statement as part of its "foundational assumptions."
What I see in the 2012 vision is a clarion-call to place the tenets of
historic and classic Christianity at the center of the theological conversations at Baylor. Therefore, I stand in sharp disagreement with
Gilbreath. What is at the heart of Baptist faith is certainly *not* "free
will" nor even the "priesthood of the believer."[13] These are the attitudes and postures with which we approach matters of faith; yet too
often they are used as the mantra for people to "believe whatever they
will as long as they believe it with all their heart." The great Baptist
founders would never have stretched their notion of the freedom of
conscience this far.[14] Rather, what lies at the heart of Baptist faith is

what lies at the heart of *all* Christian faiths that stand squarely within the historic and classic Christian tradition. I take this to be the central message of the 2012 statement. And what are those teachings?

The Christian character of Baylor is best expressed by the Great Tradition of the Christian faith, which, in the words of our colleague, Daniel Williams, "is that fundamental Christian identity for every believer no matter which of the traditions—Protestant, Roman Catholic, or Orthodox—he or she may profess."[15] These core convictions are what some in the early church spoke of as the "Rule of Faith." The Rule of Faith was a flexible but coherent body of oral teaching, derived, so the church fathers believed, from apostolic teaching and preaching. The Rule also included the moving of the Spirit in the life of the church and its elders, which meant that there was a strong understanding of how the faith develops providentially in history; in other words, the Rule of Faith is the result of Scripture and the Spirit's guidance in the life of the church.[16] At one point, Irenaeus spells out the Rule of Faith:

> The Church, though dispersed throughout the whole world, even to the ends of the earth, has received from the apostles and their disciples this faith: [she believes] in one God, the Almighty, maker of heaven and earth, and the sea, and all things that are in them; and in one Christ Jesus, Son of God, who became incarnate for our salvation; and in the Holy Spirit, who proclaimed through the prophets the dispensations of God, and the advents, and the birth from a virgin, and the passion, and the resurrection from the dead, and the ascension into heaven . . and his [future] manifestation from heaven in the glory of the Father.[17]

These core convictions are what Jonathan Edwards called the "great things of the Gospel"; they comprise what C. S. Lewis, following the Puritan Richard Baxter, referred to as "mere Christianity." We might also speak of the "Grand Christian Narrative"—the canonical plot of God's involvement in human history from Creation to Consummation—to which these doctrinal statements give specific articulation.[18]

These confessions serve a particular function, as Williams reminds us: "Like guideposts along a precipitous mountain pass, the consensual creeds and theological writings of patristic Christianity were meant to mark the path of doctrinal trustworthiness and theological constancy, as they still do, for every subsequent generation of pilgrims."[19]

The foundational assumptions and core convictions found in Baylor 2012 should be viewed as an articulation and application of the Rule of Faith or the "great things of the Gospel" appropriate to an institution of higher education aspiring to ground itself in a Baptist vision of the classic Christian tradition. Thus, I take very seriously the 2012 Mission Statement's goal to draw upon "the full range of Christian traditions" for its faculty.

But this "full range" is circumscribed by the Tradition. That is, in its hiring practices, Baylor should strive to hire Baptists, Catholics, Methodists, or Presbyterians, not as a way to "celebrate" denominational differences but as part of its efforts to enrich its Christian character. Baylor should seek to hire faculty who are a "certain kind" of Baptist, a "certain kind" of Catholic, a "certain kind" of Methodist, a "certain kind" of Presbyterian—"scholar-teachers all who, despite their denominational affiliation, embrace heartily the essentials of the Christian faith and reflect it in their lives."[20] A great Christian university cannot be built on the back of Baptists alone. It will take faculty representing the full range of the Christian traditions to accomplish this lofty goal, including non-Baptist appointments to the faculty of the Religion Department.[21]

What separates Baylor from the large majority of Christian colleges and universities that share these core convictions is the Baptist style with which Baylor applies these foundational assumptions and core convictions, that is its attitude and posture toward the implementation of these convictions in its employment practices. It would be historically 'unbaptistic' to force employees to sign any creed or lifestyle statement as a condition of employment. This fact sets Baylor apart from other robustly Christian colleges and universities (e.g., Calvin College and Wheaton College). This clearly has been the position of past administrations as well as the current administration under President Sloan and Provost Schmeltekopf, and will by all indications continue under David Jeffrey.[22] Given the recent SBC conflict, while I disagree with Gilbreath's reading of the 2012 document, I do understand his concerns, and I admit that few if any Baptist colleges or universities have succeeded in being explicitly confessional without becoming creedal.[23] But that should not stop us from trying!

The Implications for Hiring, Tenure, and Promotion:
The Significant Contribution Model

Having established some parameters for understanding what we mean when we speak of the "Baptist and Christian Character of Baylor," we turn our attention in the next section to the "Significant Contribution Model" for matters of hiring, tenure, and promotion at Baylor University.

In 1994, Thomas Flint, Professor of Philosophy at Notre Dame, presented a paper entitled "Thoughts on the Evaluation of Faculty at Notre Dame" in which he proposed that the Significant Contribution Model be used in faculty hiring, renewal, tenure, and promotion at Notre Dame.[24] Flint defines the Significant Contribution Model as a way of determining whether or not faculty have "contributed in a significant manner" to attaining the goal, in Notre Dame's case, of "creating a dynamic Catholic academic institution."[25] Flint contrasts the SCM with what he claims was the (then) current practice at Notre Dame, what he calls the "Check the Box Method," in which "being a Catholic is viewed simply as an affirmative action category—rather like being African-American or being a woman. When hiring, departments and colleges are to make special efforts to see to it that a sizable proportion (sometimes labeled a predominance) of those hired identify themselves as Catholics" presumably on some standard form that would accompany a candidate's application.[26]

Certainly, the situation of Baylor in 2003 is not the same as it was at Notre Dame in 1993-1994. In the remainder of this essay, however, I wish to propose that the SCM, properly adapted for our context, is a useful model for achieving the religious goal of Baylor 2012, to make Baylor a premier "Baptist and Christian University." It is my contention that the SCM is already tacitly in place at Baylor, so my paper is not a call to implement this model, but rather to recognize its existence and articulate more clearly its expectations.

A brief rehearsal of the hiring practices at Baylor in its recent history, beginning with the arbitrary date of 1985, will establish this thesis. Baylor used a "Fill in the Blank" Model rather than "Check the Box," but the results were the same (see Appendix 1).[27] On line 6, just below the "Degree Status" is the "Statement of Religious Commitment," in which the candidate presumably stated his or her denominational affiliation, if there was one. Note also "Checklist Item" #2 for "Recommendations/Approval for Appointment": "Was a Southern Baptist sought? If not secured, was an evangelical Christian sought?"

(The use of the word "secured" gives new meaning to the doctrine of the "security of the saints"!) At this time, there is nothing in the files regarding any kind of religious statement on the candidate's part, and anecdotal evidence suggests that, with the exception of the religion department, theological matters rarely arose during interviews with the central administration.

Also at this time, a letter was sent from the office of the President to potential faculty members, referring to Baylor's affiliation with the Baptist General Convention of Texas and claiming: "Christianity is best manifested in a loving relationship with other members of the community. This is accomplished through a caring, sharing and compassionate attitude where the full dignity of the individual as God's creation is recognized" (see Appendix 2). What is Christian about Baylor in this view is the caring, nurturing Christian context within which education at Baylor takes place. The notion that the Christian character of the University might have anything to say about the shape and content of the educational curriculum is nowhere on the horizon. The substance of this presentation does not dramatically change over the next decade (see Appendix 3). [28]

The first noticeable change in this "fill in the blank" method occurred with the appointment of Donald Schmeltekopf as chief academic officer. At least as far back as 1992, while the "fill in the blank" form was still in effect, Schmeltekopf began to append to candidates' files handwritten notes that he took during applicant interviews (See Appendix 4). By April 1994, the change in format indicates that this dimension of inquiring about the shape and expression of the candidate's religious convictions had been formalized as part of the interview process (e.g., the forms now contain a reference number in the top right hand corner; see Appendix 5). By 1996, the "Religious Affiliation Form," still used today, was in place (Appendix 6).

The election of Robert Sloan as President in the Spring 1995 ushered in many changes, including a significantly revised letter from the President's office to prospective faculty candidates. While the Sloan letter continued the emphasis on the Christian environment of the Reynolds letter, there was a significant and new element now introduced into the mix:

> Baylor University can remain true to its heritage only by recruiting, hiring, and developing faculty members who are committed as academic professionals to all the rigors of higher education ... while also being individuals who sincerely espouse and seek to express

their academic and professional identities through the particularity of the Christian faith . . . We believe that our mission as an institution of Christian higher education demands both the unfettered pursuit of all the truths of creation and also a thoughtful attempt to understand those hard won truths within a world view which finds its consummation in Jesus Christ (Appendix 7).

This explicit emphasis of the impact of the Christian intellectual tradition on the content of what faculty teach and publish was also pursued in faculty interviews and tenure procedures. Today prospective faculty are regularly asked to reflect on how they see themselves fitting into the mission of the university (Appendix 8). The official document for "Faculty Search Procedures" (approved May, 1996 upon the recommendation of the Faculty Senate, the Council of Deans, and the Provost: see Appendix 8) stipulates that on-campus candidates be sent, among other things, a copy of the Baylor University mission statement and insists:

When candidates are interviewed at the departmental, school, and university levels, officials of the University will assure that the interview includes a discussion of both the academic and the Christian dimensions of Baylor University's mission and an exploration of how the candidate can contribute to furthering that mission.[29]

In fact, many faculty finalists currently prepare written responses to the 2012 document, which has, it seems, replaced *de facto* the Baylor mission statement. And Section III.C.1.c.7 of the *Baylor Faculty Handbook* requires faculty members, as part of the tenure letter, to indicate how they have supported the "goals and mission of the University," presumably including, but not limited to, its religious mission.[30]

In this context, all of the elements of the Significant Contribution Model are currently in place. What remains is for the university to articulate more clearly its expectations in terms of hiring, tenure, and promotion.

In the case of hiring junior level faculty, the question might be framed in terms of the candidate's *potential* for making a significant contribution and his or her *willingness* to do so. Most graduate programs, including religious studies, do not address issues of integrating faith with academic study. We would do well to look beyond the immediate answers given by the newly minted Ph.D. who has had little opportunity formally to reflect on the impact of her faith on her discipline to imagine if there is promise for integration of faith and learning should the candidate be placed in an environment where such issues were pursued. Senior administrators acknowledge this point: "The candidate might be a person who, because of his or her field, hasn't had much chance for active theological reflection of a formal kind, but that would not count against them."[31] For the foreseeable future, the Baylor 2012 statement would seem the most logical document to which candidates and faculty might be asked to respond. Its wide-ranging exploration of the various ways in which Baylor's religious character is expressed through faculty research, teaching, service, and student relationships provides ample space for the prospective or current faculty member to find himself or herself and to articulate a coherent plan for contributing to this mission.

No doubt the proposal to this point raises many legitimate questions and concerns, including the following: 1) What is the relationship of the academic side of the equation to this religious dimension? 2) What do we mean by "significant contribution"; in other words, how would or could the contribution be quantified? 3) In the SCM, how do we account for the different ways in which faculty from different disciplines might make this "significant contribution"? 4) Is the significant contribution a necessary condition for hiring or tenure? 5) Who determines these expectations of the faculty member's contribution to the religious mission? The first two questions are a matter of definition and nuance. The next two press the question of how much variation in the implementation of the SCM is appropriate. And the last question addresses the matter of process and procedure.

1) *What is the relationship of the academic side of the equation to this religious dimension?* We speak a lot around Baylor about "raising the bar" on the academic side, especially in terms of faculty research, and there is a great deal of debate about whether or not one can be both an active researcher AND a stellar classroom teacher.[32] I simply wish to observe that both sides of the bar—the academic AND the religious—have been raised. Just as the research component has gone from the perception of "scholarship tolerated" (or even, according to some sources, "scholarship discouraged") to "scholarship encouraged" to "scholarship expected" to now "scholarship required," so the expectation of the faculty member's stance toward Baylor's religious character has gone from "comfortable with the religious mission" to "sympathetic toward" to "supportive of" to now finally "contributing to" the religious mission.[33] It seems to me that both sides of

the bar should be raised in this way because to raise one side without raising the other will, to put it starkly, lead either to secularism, on the one hand, or vacuous pietism, on the other.[34] Imperative III of the 2012 statement makes the goal explicit: "We will recruit high-potential junior faculty and highly esteemed senior faculty who embrace the Christian faith and are knowledgeable of the Christian intellectual tradition. Many of these faculty will especially exemplify the integration of faith and learning in their disciplines and in interdisciplinary or collaborative activities."[35]

2) *What do we mean by "significant contribution"? How would or could it be quantified?* If we thought it difficult to quantify expectations of scholarly contributions, imagine the problems potentially associated with measuring what constitutes a faculty member's "significant contribution" to Baylor's religious character.

Nonetheless, recognizing such a task to be more of an art than a science, there are some avenues of inquiry one would want to pursue to determine whether or not a faculty member could help (in the case of hiring) or is helping (in the case of tenure) make Baylor a more vibrant Christian intellectual center. In terms of hiring, we might ask: Does the candidate have a sense of vocation shaped by her Christian commitments? Are the candidate's research projects, if relevant, influenced in some way by his or her Christian belief? Are the topics he or she investigates ones of special and pressing interest to Christians? Where possible, does the candidate pursue a distinctively Christian approach to topics of more general interest within the discipline in question? With regard to teaching, how does the candidate see Christianity as fitting in? Will the issues approached or the perspectives offered by the candidate contribute in some special way to our students' growth as Christian intellectuals?[36] One could then imagine returning to these and similar questions when evaluating the tenure candidate's contribution to the religious mission. The difficulty in shaping generic questions is no doubt in part due to disciplinary differences. As Flint notes, the "precise questions one ought to ask an accountant might well be different from those properly addressed to a philosopher."[37] This point leads us to our next question.

3) *In the SCM, how do we account for the different ways in which faculty from different disciplines might make this "significant contribution"?* From the beginning, critics have pointed to the disparity in the degree to which faculty from different disciplines could engage in issues of faith and learning; say the differences between scholarship in the humanities and that in the hard sciences. Schmeltekopf, at the

beginning of his second year as Vice President for Academic Affairs, made a remarkable address before the Board of Regents entitled "Reflections on the Future of Baylor as a Christian University." This address, given on July 16, 1992, anticipated many of the arguments that have unfolded over the last ten years. On this matter, Schmeltekopf wrote: "All of the disciplines of the humanities and the arts can readily be connected with this grand scholarly Christian tradition. But perhaps you are wondering how a branch of knowledge such as chemistry or mathematics can 'be informed by and infused with 'Christian beliefs.' As far as I know, there is no such discipline as 'Christian chemistry' or 'evangelical Christian mathematics.'"[38] Thus, it might be difficult for some faculty or prospective candidates to imagine how they might make *any* contribution to the religious mission of the university, much less a "significant" one.

To address this question, it might be helpful to consider Stephen Evans's proposal regarding what constitutes Christian scholarship. According to Evans, central to any definition of Christian scholarship is the notion of vocation, where the scholar understands her scholarship as an act of devotion to God rather than an exercise in self-aggrandizement or in praise of human intellect.[39] Furthermore, Evans distinguishes three kinds of "Christian scholarship": explicit Christian scholarship, implicit Christian scholarship, and purely vocational Christian scholarship. Explicit Christian scholarship "wears its Christian character on its sleeve, and is intended as a form of Christian apologetics and testimony."[40] Much of the work in our seminary, religion department, and philosophy department would fall into this category. We might find implicit Christian scholarship in the fields of psychology, sociology, art history, literature, and law where the author's Christian faith has shaped both the choice of the issue to be studied and the hypotheses being tested, although the methodology itself is not distinctively or necessarily "Christian." Purely vocational scholarship has nothing about it—explicit or implicit—that is distinctly Christian. Rather, the Christian mathematician or the Christian chemist constructs the same proofs or conducts the same experiments as the non-Christian. Yet the Christian scientist "bears witness to the Kingdom of God," and Christian scientists do so "simply by doing excellent work in their disciplines, contributing to the development of new knowledge, furthering the general good, and also demonstrating that it is indeed possible for a thoughtful, educated person to live as a Christian in today's world."[41]

Evans then puts forward what he calls a "relevance continuum" intended to demonstrate that "as one goes from the left to the right the impact that Christian faith has on a question in particular discipline becomes more and more common."

(less) _____ *(more)*
Mathematics Natural Sciences Human Sciences History Literature/Arts Philosophy/Theology

Evans explains, "The number of questions where faith will divide believers from non-believers is fewer as one goes to the left; the amount of common ground and the ease of finding it is smaller as one goes to the right, though it never vanishes altogether. Even in philosophy and theology there are many questions about which onc[']s ultimate faith commitment will make no difference."[42]

However, this point should not be used to discourage the new exploration of connections between the Christian intellectual tradition and various disciplines where such connections have not historically been found. To quote Flint again:

> [W]e would not simply endorse the assumption common at our secular peer institutions that Christianity has very limited ramifications for serious academic research and teaching. . . . in many other fields, I suspect, connections will be uncovered if we look; and in those fields, to ignore completely the issue of significant contribution would not be conducive to our principal institutional goals.[43]

Furthermore, this concession does not mean that the faculty member would not, as a member of the Baylor community of scholars, contribute meaningfully to the larger campus discussions and debates.

4) *Is the significant contribution a necessary condition for hiring or tenure?* Fulfilling the expectation of making a significant contribution to the religious character might well be considered as *necessary* for hiring, tenure, and promotion. This is especially true for the "relevance continuum" model, since it is understood that "Christian scholarship is not monolithic but pluralistic, reflecting the diversity of Christians and their vocations."[44] Thus, those who are engaged in "purely vocational" Christian scholarship do so in a self-conscious effort to honor God, and they will do so in part by producing first-rate scholarship which endures the most rigorous examination by their expert peers. Thus, while a significant contribution (or the potential thereof) would be a necessary condition for hiring, tenure, and

promotion, what counts as "Christian scholarship" is defined broadly enough to make room for all who are making a self-conscious effort to honor God through their scholarship.

Departments whose disciplines tend to fall on the "left" side of the continuum might want to consider developing guidelines whereby candidates for hiring or tenure would participate in brown bag lunch groups, faculty orientation and workshops, and guest lectures where matters of what it means to be a Christian professor could be discussed and debated.[45]

5) *Who determines these expectations of the faculty member's contribution to the religious mission?* Baptists prize democratic governance, and dissent is another long cherished Baptist ideal.[46] Thus, the issues raised here should be the subject of vigorous but civil debate. And we do have some good models for such discourse at the university. Recently, at least in my experience in the Religion Department, there has been healthy and mutual exchange between the faculty and the central administration on establishing the guidelines for tenure.

I would submit that since this process is still ongoing, the conversation be extended to include the formulation of an explicit statement of the expectations for faculty in light of Baylor's religious character. This procedure should allow, as it has up to this point, for each departmental unit, with its own local culture, to engage in dialogue with the central administration. The questions I have posed here could provide some initial focus to those discussions. If uniformity of the SCM is beyond our grasp, some coherence might nonetheless be achieved. To ignore totally the implications of the religious character of the institution on the issues of hiring, tenure, and promotion, however, is to invite failure, perhaps even disaster, in our efforts to fulfill what is Baylor's unique mission: to become the premier Christian university in the Protestant tradition.

Conclusion

I have attempted here, for the sake of analysis, to separate principle from practice, policy from implementation. Obviously, this is a difficult task and might strike some to be as futile an undertaking as "unscrambling an egg." Nonetheless, more clearly understood principles may lead to more judicious practices.

Both Drs. Sloan and Schmeltekopf have used the opening faculty meeting of the fall semester as an opportunity to outline their goals and aspirations for the future of Baylor University. Many of the ideas we see in the 2012 document were first broached in that context. In the second of four such addresses Schmeltekopf asserted:

> I believe Baylor is at a crossroads in its history. . . . The alternatives open to us can be put simply: We can either maintain our present course, with appropriate fine-tuning along the way, or we can aspire to much higher levels of accomplishment and thereby become an academically and intellectually powerful university indeed, one of the top two or three Christian universities in the world.[47]

All indications suggest that we have, in fact, moved past the crossroads and are moving with all due haste down the second, more ambitious path. We have been helped by folks like Don Schmeltekopf who have led the way, clearing the path of the overgrowth of fuzzy and short-sighted thinking. For this, and for him, we should all be grateful! *Gloria Deo!*[48]

Notes

[1] I doubt Dr. Schmeltekopf will remember our first encounter; it was not in an academic context. Rather, at the beginning of the first semester that Dr. Schmeltekopf came to Baylor as Vice Provost, he and I played doubles together at the YMCA. He had a hard serve, aggressive net game, and a relentless desire to win! While both of us have aged over the ensuing dozen years or so (actually only I have aged!), some things never change. The second encounter I remember most vividly was the beginning of the fall semester after Don had been named Provost. He came to the Religion Department faculty retreat held in the Alumni center and began to lay out his vision for the Religion Department's role in Baylor's becoming a great "Christian University." That talk made a profound and lasting impact on me, as I know it did on others (having heard President Sloan mention publicly this same meeting on several occasions). Much of what he said I had never heard nor thought of before, this despite the fact that from the day I entered college as a freshman until the day, nine years later, when I crossed the stage to receive my Doctor of Philosophy degree, my entire educational career had been spent at Baptist institutions of learning. Indeed, much of the expenses of my education were underwritten by ordinary Baptists giving their tithes and offerings to the Cooperative Program. Over the past twelve years, by engaging in countless conversations with colleagues (many of them patiently instigated and guided by my good friend Michael Beaty), by listening attentively to a parade of Christian intellectuals who discoursed about the topic (folks like Nicholas Wolterstorff, George Marsden, and Nancy

Ammerman), and by reading sporadically in the field, I came to the conclusion that Baylor University as a premier Christian university was not only a realistic, but a wholly desirable goal.

[2] Walter Shurden, one of the doyens of Baptist history, used the term "style" to refer to the Baptist perspective on matters of faith: "So I settled on 'freedom' and used the word to describe, not a single Baptist distinctive, but a specific *style* of faith, a distinctive *posture* of faith, a particular *attitude* toward the issues of faith" (my emphasis). See Walter B. Shurden, "The Baptist Identity and the Baptist Manifesto," *Perspectives in Religious Studies*, 25 (1998): 323-324 fn. 7. See also Shurden, *The Baptist Identity: Four Fragile Freedoms* (Macon, GA: Smyth & Helwys, 1993). Furthermore, a recent collection of nine pamphlets were released by the William H. Whitsitt Baptist Heritage Society in conjunction with Baptist History and Heritage entitled *The Baptist Style for a New Century: Documents for Faith and Witness* (eds. Charles DeWeese and Walter Shurden, 2001). Appreciation is expressed to Douglas Weaver for drawing this publication to my attention.

[3] Baylor 2012: Ten Year Vision, 22.

[4] I understand that the situation I describe in the following paragraphs is not the situation at many Baptist colleges and universities, where the real threat to academic integrity remains on the religious right. Since the charter change of 1991, however, this has not, in my opinion, been the major threat for Baylor University. On the charter change, see Michael Beaty and Larry Lyon, "Baylor's Great Conflict and Herbert Reynolds' Great Victory," *No Little Plans: The Leadership and Legacy of Herbert Reynolds* (Narrative Publishing Company: Waco, Texas, 2000) 57-79.

[5] Paraphrasing Shlomith Rimmon-Kenan, *Narrative Fiction: Contemporary Poetics* (London: Methuen, 1983) 127.

[6] See especially the now well-known arguments of George Marsden, *The Soul of the American University: From Protestant Establishment to Established Nonbelief* (New York: Oxford University Press, 1994); James Tunstead Burtchaell, *The Dying of the Light: The Disengagement of Colleges and Universities from Their Christian Churches* (Grand Rapids: Eerdmans, 1998).

[7] Thomas Helwys, *A Short Declaration of the Mystery of Iniquity*, ed. Richard Groves (Macon, GA: Mercer University Press, 1998) 53.

[8] See, for example, the recent address, "Religious Heritage and Academic Culture at Wake Forest," by Dr. Thomas Hearn, President of Wake Forest University, on September, 24, 2002, on the inauguration of the Pro Humanitate, a Lilly Foundation funded initiative on the "Theological Exploration of Vocation." Hearn highlights "freedom" as the hallmark Baptist distinctive that has shaped Wake Forest over the years:

> So in honoring this religious heritage and in claiming this part of our corporate personality, Wake Forest acknowledges an element of our past which directed us at critical moments to choose freedom — academic freedom,

freedom of expression, and freedom of religion — with all of the controversy that freedom engenders. This is not a history to be overcome or set aside. This is a history to be prized and nurtured." Elsewhere he claims: "I hasten to add that this religious posture is compatible with our respect for religious pluralism and the desire, even the necessity, that we hear and heed different and dissenting voices. At one level, this is because we are devoted to learning from others the alternative ways in which transcendence has been construed. But in purely religious terms, the Baptist insistence that there is no prescribed orthodox code of belief — no creed — means that we must all posit the propositions of faith with humility and the recognition that we cannot contain divine truth in human formulations. Each person being a priest means that no one person can affirm his or her own faith formula as divinely ordained. We live and we walk by faith.

[9] Gilbreath, "Baylor 2012: A Vision Re-examined," (Essay 2-R) 1.

[10] Gilbreath, "A Vision Re-examined," 1.

[11] From the website of Criswell College at http: //www.criswell.edu/.

[12] *Baylor 2012*, "Foundational Assumptions."

[13] Gilbreath's very formulation, "the priesthood of the believer" (in the singular), rather than "the priesthood of ALL believers" (the plural being the language of our Baptist ancestors) implies a fundamental misunderstanding of the doctrine; on this see especially, Timothy George, "The Priesthood of All Believers," *The People of God: Essays on the Believers' Church*, eds. David Dockery and Paul Basden (Nashville: Broadman, 1991) 85-95.

[14] Walter Shurden has forcefully made this point even while arguing that these Baptist convictions led to theological diversity rather than conformity: "To say that their convictions encouraged diversity does not suggest in the least that Baptists had no firm certainties regarding cardinal Christian truths, nor is it to say that their opinions were flabby with an 'anything goes' approach to the Bible and theology. They were as certain, even dogmatic, about their views as the most fervent bishop in the Church of England" ("How We Got That Way: Baptists on Religious Liberty and Separation of Church and State," Address presented at the Sixtieth Celebration of the Baptist Joint Committee, 8 October 1996, Washington, DC, 5).

[15] Daniel H. Williams, *Retrieving the Tradition and Renewing Evangelicalism* (Grand Rapids: Eerdmans, 1999) 7.

[16] The Rule also included the moving of the Spirit in the life of the church and its elders, which meant that there was a strong providential understanding of how the faith develops in history; in other words, the Rule of faith is the result of Scripture and the Spirit's guidance in the life of the church. For more on the role of the Rule of Faith in Protestant interpretation of scripture, see especially C. Stephen Evans, "Tradition, Biblical Interpretation, and Historical Truth," *"Behind" the Text: History and Biblical Interpretation*, ed. Craig Bartholomew, Mary Healy, C. Stephen Evans, and Murrae Rae (Grand Rapids: Zondervan,

2003); D. Jeffrey Bingham, "Evangelicals, Irenaeus, and the Bible," *The Free Church and the Early Church: Bridging the Historical and Theological Divide*, ed. Daniel H. Williams (Grand Rapids: Eerdmans, 2002) 27-46.

[17] Irenaeus, *Against Heresies*, I.10 (Ante-Nicene Fathers, I. 330); cited by Williams, *Retrieving the Tradition*, 89.

[18] These core convictions would be those that originate from the Christian Scriptures and are manifested in various expressions through the creeds, and clarified and interpreted by the Ecumenical Councils through the Magisterial Reformers.

[19] Williams, *Retrieving the Tradition*, 172.

[20] The language is that of my colleague, Dean Martin, from an email dated 4 February 2003, in response to an earlier version of this paper.

[21] I do not intend this statement as a weakening of the resolve to have Baptists only in the religion department, but as a recognition of the reality that there are certain areas in the classic theological disciplines, essential for the curriculum of a doctoral-granting, comprehensive university, in which Baptists are historically underrepresented. The recent faculty surveys of Notre Dame, Boston College, Brigham Young, and Baylor University by Larry Lyon, Michael Beaty, and Stephanie Litizzette Mixon, "Making Sense of a 'Religious' University: Faculty Adaptations and Opinions at Brigham Young, Baylor, Notre Dame, and Boston College," *Review of Religious Research*, 43 (2002): 326-348 suggest that faculty who are members of the sponsoring church of the university are typically much more supportive of the religious mission of the university than are their counterparts (non-Catholics at Notre Dame or Boston College, non-Baptists at Baylor University). In light of this evidence, it would seem that Baylor must maintain a significant percentage of administrators, faculty, and staff, who identify with and are grounded in the Baptist vision of Christianity. These surveys were conducted in the mid-90s; it would be interesting to see what effect the recent hiring practices at Baylor have had on the attitudes of non-Baptist Baylor faculty toward the religious character of the institution. On occasion, the Board of Regents has also affirmed that Baylor can hire a "certain kind of Jew" to contribute to the university's mission.

[22] Dr. Jeffrey affirmed this position in a recent article:

> "At Calvin College, faculty must sign a long series of statements of faith, agree to attend the Christian Reform Church, and send their children to the Christian Reform school," Jeffrey says. "At Wheaton College, faculty must sign a statement of faith, a statement of doctrine, and a code of behavior," he notes. "But Baylor says you can come in here from any denomination you want. We're not concerned with that, although I think almost half of Baylor faculty hires are Baptists," Jeffrey says. "Do we ask them to sign a statement of faith? No. Do we have them sign a statement of behavior? No. Do we require them to belong to a Baptist church? No."

Meg Cullar, "Creating the Faculty of the Future," *Baylor Line,* Winter 2003: 35-43.

[23] Consider the most recent example of Palm Beach Atlantic University reported by the state newspaper, *Florida Baptist Witness*, 120 (January 16, 2003). Interim President Ken Mahanes reportedly drafted a statement of faith, which, effective with the 2003-2004 academic year, all faculty *and* all trustees must affirm. The statement includes the typical buzz words of "infallible" Scriptures and Christ's "vicarious and atoning death" and a curious reference to the "resurrection of damnation."

[24] I am grateful to Donald Schmeltekopf for sharing some of these unpublished papers with me, and to Thomas Flint for giving me a copy of his paper and rejoinder to the responses. Citations are from those unpublished manuscripts with the author's permission.

[25] Flint 3.

[26] Flint 2.

[27] I wish to express gratitude to the Provost's office by providing copies of the materials used in the Appendixes.

[28] Note, however, that in pre-charter change 1985 Baylor is "closely affiliated" with the BGCT and in 1995 only "affiliated with"!

[29] There is also attached in the document the following caveat: "The recommendations contained in this document address particular procedures in the faculty search process and should not be interpreted as an exclusive description of all the policies and procedures involved in faculty searches."

[30] 2002-03 Baylor Faculty Handbook, 119.

[31] *Baylor Line,* Winter 2003: 42, quoting David Jeffrey. For mid-to senior-level appointments, the candidates might reasonably be expected to demonstrate ways in which they are already prepared to contribute to Baylor's religious mission. Just as we might be skeptical of a mid-career candidate who lays out an ambitious research agenda, but who has no proven track record of publications, so we might wonder about the candidate who, in the middle of his career, was unable to demonstrate "an interest in what we would call basic issues that involve faith—moral issues, ethical issues, issues about suffering. If they didn't have any, I would probably think—and you would, too—that it really doesn't . . . much matter to them or they would have thought about it."

[32] See the recent lead article, Jason Embry, "BU wants faculty with the write stuff," *Waco Tribune-Herald*, 9 Feb. 2003: 1A, 8A.

[33] Of course, individual faculty members were engaged in leading research or making significant contributions to Baylor's religious character prior to the current administration. The shift is intended to describe the general *ethos* of the overall campus at the time.

[34] On the negative impact of American Pietism on Christian colleges and universities, see especially the last chapter of Burtchaell's *Dying of the Light*. On maintaining both the academic and religious aspects of a Christian University,

see Michael Beaty, Todd Buras, and Larry Lyon, "Christian Higher Education: An Historical and Philosophical Perspective," *Perspectives in Religious Studies*, 24 (1997): 145-166.

[35] *Baylor 2012*, "Imperative III: Develop a World-Class Faculty."

[36] These questions are modified from Flint, "Thoughts," 6.

[37] Flint, "Thoughts," 5.

[38] Donald Schmeltekopf, "Reflections on the Future of Baylor as a Christian University," address given before the Board of Regents, 16 July 1992.

[39] C. Stephen Evans, "The Calling of the Christian-Scholar Teacher," *The Southern Baptist Educator*, LXIII 4 (1999): 4.

[40] Evans, "Christian Scholarship and the Biblical Drama," *The Southern Baptist Educator*, LXIV 1 (1999): 3.

[41] Evans, "Christian Scholarship and the Biblical Drama," 3.

[42] Evans, "Christian Scholarship and the Biblical Drama," 5.

[43] Thomas Flint, "Reply to Gutting and Hamburg," 4. Jeffrey, *Baylor Line*: 40, makes a similar point: "We ask them [faculty candidates] to tell us about their own spiritual pilgrimages. . . . And then we ask them if this makes any difference in how they think about the world and how they think about scholarship. . . . I think it would be fair to say that we're more particularly interested in those areas where there are obvious connections to faith—like religion, philosophy, history, and so on. But we ask the question of everybody, and we get such interesting and surprising answers."

[44] Evans, "Christian Scholarship and the Biblical Drama," 3. Evans goes on to say: "Christian scholars will not agree on everything and that is not necessarily a bad thing. Thus, there is room within Christian scholarship for Christian feminism, Christian conservatism, Christian romanticism, etc. However, it is important to remember what is *absolute* and what is *relative*, what is ultimately important and what is only important."

[45] Such activities would then count as part of the faculty's significant contribution, and could even be quantified if that were desirable (e.g., a faculty is expected to have participated "X" number of hours in such "mission-serving" activities along the way to tenure, where "X" is determined by the department and central administration) .

[46] On President Sloan's affirmation of the indispensability of debate for the community of scholars at the university, see "Change and Collegiality in the Community of Scholars," delivered at the general faculty meeting, 14 Jan. 2003.

> Community truly is important because we need the testing, the honing, the sharpening of iron against iron that by definition only a community can give, and, we need the nurturing and support to risk, to dare, to think, and thus, the freedom to fail and be wrong that likewise only community can give.The inevitable stresses of engagement in response to the clash of fiercely held ideas and the freedom of unfettered conversation in pursuit of

the truth presuppose a community of trust and mutual respect as the indispensable environment where such encounters may productively take place. As a Christian institution, we unapologetically adopt a frame of reference, even a set of intellectual traditions, which we call our own. Above all, we take seriously the gospel center of our faith, seeking to understand the cross of Jesus, his resurrection, and our confession that He is Lord within the framework of our particular calling and context as an institution of higher learning. But, precisely because we confess that he is Lord over all things visible and invisible, we are called to engage and understand the world, its peoples and its ways. Our stewardship is to bring "every thought captive to Christ." But because we are called to live by faith and with humility we cannot know ahead of time where these battles of the mind and heart will lead. We will not always agree about what we see and how we interpret it. Indeed, oftentimes our disagreements are what animate our intellectual lives and inform our scholarship. We will disagree—even as we seek the same truth. We will debate the facts—even as we confront the same realities. We will certainly differ in working out the implications of the one confession "Jesus Christ is Lord." But, we must do so as a community of scholars: a place where trust, integrity, humility, and mutual respect abound.

Nonetheless, a strong central administration, anchored by robust Presidential leadership, is essential to the success of any faith-related institution of higher education seeking to retain its religious heritage in a meaningful way. Both George Marsden, "The Soul of the American University" and Burtchaell, "The Alienation of Christian Higher Education in America: Diagnosis and Prognosis," *Schooling Christians: "Holy Experiments" in American Higher Education*, ed. Stanley Hauerwas and John H. Westerhoff (Grand Rapids: Eerdmans, 1992) esp. 149 make it clear that often the Christian university's path to secularization is paved by the cumulative effect of the University President's unintentional, but nonetheless culpable, decisions and choices along the way.

[47] Donald D. Schmeltekopf, "Baylor at a Crossroads," Faculty Address, 17 August 2000.

[48] I am deeply grateful to the following persons who read all or parts of this paper (often in multiple versions) and gave helpful, often critical, feedback: Bill Bellinger, Barry Harvey, Heidi Hornik, Naymond Keathley, Bob Kruschwitz, Dean Martin, Charles Talbert, Douglas Weaver, and Ralph Wood. Especially do I owe Michael Beaty an enormous thanks. His previous writing on this subject, his pointing to various sources, and his generous critique and evaluation saved me from many errors. This paper is, in fact, the result of intensive collaboration over these ideas and concepts, though responsibility for the final product is finally mine.

Appendix 1

Ref. AFP No. _____

CANDIDATE PROPOSED FOR INTERVIEW/APPOINTMENT

This request is to be completed by Department Chairman

Department and School/College _____ Account No. _____

Position Title _____ Position No. _321_

Total number of applications received for position 45 as of (date) _____ -85

Candidate's Name _____

Last _____ First _____ M. _____ Social Security No. _3_

Degree Status: _Ph.D._ Birth Date: _____. Resume Attached: _X_ Yes ____ No Recommendations: _3_

Statement of Religious Commitment: _Baptist_

Interviewed by: _McLeod, Miller, Palf & Belew_ Date: _____

RECOMMENDATIONS/APPROVAL FOR APPOINTMENT

Checklist Items:

1. Was a nationwide search conducted of which this candidate was a part? _Yes_
2. Was a Southern Baptist sought? _yes_ If not secured, was an evangelical Christian sought? _____
3. Were federal and state Equal Employment Opportunity laws complied with? _yes_
4. Are transcripts of all college work attached? _yes_
5. Has the candidate been furnished a physical exam form for completion? _____

Recommendation/Approval of Part-time Lecturers

Proposed compensation/No. of sem. hrs./for fall, spring or academic year	Department Chairman	Date
Recommend approval/disapproval; comments	Dean of School/College	Date
Approved/disapproved; comments	VP and Provost	Date

Recommendation/Approval of Full-time Lecturers and Tenure-Track Faculty
(Signatures required only for tenure-track positions)

We, the tenured members of the faculty of the Department/School of _____ Arts and Sciences

recommend that a contract for employment be offered to _____

Proposed academic rank _AssT PROF_ _____ Proposed salary _____

	Date 3-8-85
☑ Recommend approval ☐ Recommend disapproval Comments	Robert T. Miller Department Chairman Date 3-8-85
☑ Recommend approval ☐ Recommend disapproval Comments	John S. Belew Dean of School/College Date 3/18/85
☑ Approved ☐ Disapproved Comments	Herbert H. Reynolds Vice President and Provost Date 3/18/85

Follow-up Action by Dean of Academic Services

1. Has physical exam been completed and is it clear? _yes_ Physical exam must be completed before a contract can be mailed.
2. Salary level and rank confirmed by _JSB_ HHR
3. Previous teaching credit _____ Tenure credit _____
4. Contract mailed _____ Contract returned _____
5. Remarks: _____

Original: Dean of Academic Services
Copies: Vice President and Provost
          Dean of School/College

Appendix :

Herbert H. Reynolds
President

Telephone 817-755-1311
Waco, Texas 76798

BAYLOR UNIVERSITY

1985

Dear Prospective Faculty Member:

Baylor is the oldest institution of higher learning in the State of
Texas and one of the oldest institutions of higher learning west of
the Mississippi River. We are grateful for our heritage as a strong
church-related institution and as a major university in the United
States.

Please allow me to share with you a few of the distinctives of Baylor
University to insure that you as a faculty prospect have a clear
understanding of those expectations which may lie beyond the usual
contractual requirements. The American Association of University
Professors has asked all colleges and universities to be explicit in
outlining such expectations and we feel that it is very important
that we do this at Baylor.

>   First, you will find that Baylor is distinctive in its
>   sense of community. In my opinion, our faculty, staff
>   and students comprise one of the finest groups of
>   people with whom I have ever been associated. We
>   genuinely seek a strong sense of community to promote
>   harmonious and wholesome relationships with students,
>   colleagues and the administration.
>
>   Second, we were founded by Baptists in early 1845 and
>   we have been closely affiliated with the Baptist
>   General Convention of Texas during our entire exist-
>   ence. We thus take our church-relatedness quite
>   seriously. We believe that we are privileged to con-
>   tribute to the pluralism in higher education as we
>   strive to develop our students in the spiritual realm
>   along with their mental development. Christianity at
>   Baylor is best manifested in a loving relationship with
>   other members of the community. This is accomplished
>   through a caring, sharing and compassionate attitude
>   where the full dignity of the individual as God's crea-
>   tion is recognized. We certainly do not seek to sub-
>   stitute piety for the kind of strong academic program
>   and academic standards we are committed to at Baylor.
>   On the contrary, we believe that our strongest witness
>   as a Christian institution comes from excelling in
>   every phase of University life.

-2-

Third, and last, you will be expected to be a well-prepared and excellent teacher in the classroom, a publishing scholar if you choose to take advantage of available programs for faculty development, and we will appreciate your involvement in University life through committees and various study groups.

In summary, should you join us I believe that you will be most happy at Baylor if you conduct yourself in a professional fashion, if you are committed to Christian moral principles, if you are well-prepared for your teaching and seek to do a first-rate job of teaching, if you are interested in being a scholarly person and taking advantage of faculty development programs, and if you will work harmoniously along with your colleagues in various University endeavors to be a part of the governing structure and contribute to the furtherance of the University. Our students will be the ultimate beneficiaries of your effectiveness and you will receive the kind of psychic and material rewards that should make life meaningful for you. If you do join us at Baylor I shall look forward to working with you and helping you to fulfill your professional and personal goals.

Cordially yours,

Herbert H. Reynolds
President

cd

Appendix 3

BAYLOR
U N I V E R S I T Y

1995

Dear Prospective Faculty Member:

Baylor is the oldest institution of higher learning in the State of Texas and one of the oldest institutions of higher learning west of the Mississippi River. We are grateful that we are now recognized as the premier Baptist university in the world.

Please allow me to share with you a few of the distinctives of Baylor University to insure that you as a faculty prospect have a clear understanding of those expectations which may lie beyond the usual contractual requirements. The American Association of University Professors has asked all colleges and universities to be explicit in outlining such expectations and we feel that it is very important that we do this at Baylor.

First, we were founded by Baptists in early 1845 and are now affiliated with the Baptist General Convention of Texas. We take our church-relatedness quite seriously and we expect our faculty to embrace Christian values and high personal standards by both precept and example. Christianity at Baylor is best manifested in a loving relationship with other members of the community. This is accomplished through a caring, sharing and compassionate attitude where the full dignity of the individual as God's creation is recognized. We do not seek to substitute piety for the kind of strong academic programs and academic standards to which we are committed; on the contrary, we believe that our strongest witness as a Christian institution comes from excelling in every phase of University life.

Second, you will be expected first and foremost to be a well-prepared and excellent teacher in the classroom, a publishing scholar if you choose to take advantage of available programs for faculty development, and we will appreciate your involvement in University life through committees and various study groups.

Third, you will find that Baylor is distinctive in its sense of community. In my opinion, our faculty, staff and students comprise one of the finest groups of people with whom I have ever been associated. We genuinely seek a strong sense of community to promote harmonious and wholesome relationships among students, colleagues and the administration.

OFFICE OF THE PRESIDENT
WACO, TEXAS 76798 · (817) 755-1311

-2-

Fourth, as a religiously controlled institution of higher education Baylor is permitted to discriminate on the basis of religion. Further, because of the high moral standards expected of all members of the university community, prospective faculty should familiarize themselves with Baylor's policy on sexual misconduct as well as other matters of personal conduct involving moral issues.

In summary, should you join us I believe that you will be most happy at Baylor and most likely to gain tenure if you conduct yourself in a professional fashion, if you are committed to Christian and Baptist moral principles, if you are well-prepared and seek to do a first-rate job of teaching, if you take advantage of faculty development programs, and if you will work harmoniously with your colleagues in various University endeavors to be a part of the governing structure and contribute to the furtherance of the University. Our students will be the ultimate beneficiaries of your effectiveness and you will receive the kind of psychic and material rewards that should make life meaningful for you.

If you do join us at Baylor I shall look forward to working with you and helping you to fulfill your professional and personal goals.

Cordially yours,

Herbert H. Reynolds
President.

meb

Attachment: Purpose/Mission of Baylor University

Appendix 4

Ref. AFP No.

CANDIDATE PROPOSED FOR INTERVIEW/APPOINTMENT

This request is to be completed by Department Chair

Department _____ School/College Arts & Science

Position Title _____ Position No. _____

Total number of applications received for position ___61___ as of (date) _____

Candidate's Name _____

Degree Status: Ph.D. Birth date: _____ Resume Attached: _X_ Yes ___ No Recommendations: 3

Statement of Religious Commitment: Methodist

Interviewed by: Drs. Schmelthopf Date: ___/92

RECOMMENDATIONS/APPROVAL FOR APPOINTMENT
Checklist Items:

1. Was a nationwide search conducted of which this candidate was a part? _____yes
2. Was a Southern Baptist sought? __yes__ If not secured, was an evangelical Christian sought? __yes__
23. Were federal and state Affirmative Action/Equal Employment Opportunity laws complied with? _____
4. Was the Immigration Reform and Control Act of 1986 complied with? _____
5. Are transcripts of all college work attached? _____

Recommendation/Approval of Part-time Lecturers

Proposed compensation/No. of sem. hrs./for fall, spring or academic year	Department Chair	Date

Dean of School/College	Date	Vice President for Academic Affairs	Date

Comments

☐ Approved   ☐ Disapproved   Vice President for Administrative Affairs and COO   Date

Recommendation/Approval of Full-time Lecturers and Tenure-Track Faculty
(Signatures required only for tenure-track positions)

We, the tenured members of the faculty of the Department/School of ___Chemistry___

recommend that a contract for employment be offered to

Proposed academic rank _asst professor_ Proposed salary _____

☐ Fall   ☐ Spring   ☒ Academic Year 199 3-94   Department Chair   2-5-93 Date

Proposed credit for previous teaching _____ Tenure _____

W. F. Coyle 2/7/93   James A. Martin Jr. 2/8/93   Drs. Schmelthopf 2-9-9
Dean of School/College Date   Vice President for Academic Affairs Dept Affairs   VP for Administrative Affairs and COO Date

Comments

☒ Approved   ☐ Disapproved   President   2/17/93 Date

Follow-up Action by Dean for Academic Services

1. Salary level and rank confirmed by _____ Eligible for Annuity Program _____
2. Pretenure review _____ Consideration by University Tenure Committee _____
3. Contract mailed _____ Contract returned _____
4. Remarks: _____

Original: Assistant Dean for Academic Services
Copies: Vice President for Academic Affairs

SUMMARY OF FACULTY PROSPECT INTERVIEW

NAME:_____

POSITION:_____

DEPARTMENT/SCHOOL:_____

RELIGIOUS COMMITMENT:

Methodist

COMMENTS

is a lifelong Methodist. He spoke sincerely of his own Christian pilgrimage, from his home church in Illinois to his church participation now in (which he admitted has not been as active as he would have liked). He understands the mission of Baylor as a Christian university, and would be supportive of it.

_____   12-17-92
(Signature)   (Date)

Appendix 5

Ref. AFP No.

CANDIDATE PROPOSED FOR INTERVIEW/APPOINTMENT

This request is to be completed by Department Chair

Department _____   School/College ___Arts & Scien-

Position Title _____   Position No. _____

Total number of applications received for position ___250___   as of (date)_____

Candidate's Name _____   Social Security No.
                                  Last   9

Degree Status:__PhD.__ Birth date:_____ Resume Attached:_X_ Yes ___No   Recommendations:___

Statement of Religious Commitment:__Active Methodist__   794

Interviewed by: Dr. Schmeltekopf,Dr. Cooper _____   Date: _____

RECOMMENDATIONS/APPROVAL FOR APPOINTMENT

Checklist Items:
  1. Was a nationwide search conducted of which this candidate was a part? __Yes__
  2. Was a Southern Baptist sought? __Yes__   If not secured, was an evangelical Christian sought? __Yes__
  3. Were federal and state Affirmative Action/Equal Employment Opportunity laws complied with? __Yes__
  4. Was the Immigration Reform and Control Act of 1986 complied with? __Yes__
  5. Are transcripts of all college work attached? _____

Recommendation/Approval of Part-time Lecturers

Proposed compensation/No. of sem. hrs./for fall, spring or academic year _____   Department Chair _____   Date _____

Dean of School/College _____   Date _____   Vice President and COO for Administrative Affairs _____   Date _____

Comments _____

☐ Approved   ☐ Disapproved _____
                                           Vice President and COO for Academic Affairs _____   Date _____

Recommendation/Approval of Full-time Lecturers and Tenure-Track Faculty
(Signatures required only for tenure-track positions)

We, the tenured members of the faculty of the Department/School of Engineering and Computer Science

recommend that a contract for employment be offered to

Proposed academic rank __Assistant Professor__   Proposed salary _____

☑ Fall   ☐ Spring   ☐ Academic Year 199_4_   / Department Chair _____   Date _____

Proposed credit for previous teaching _____   Tenure _____

M. J. Cooper 5/11/94 _____ 5/23/94   Donald W. Schmeltekopf 5/23/9
Dean of School/College   Date   VP and COO for Administrative Affairs   Date   VP and COO for Academic Affairs

Comments

☑ Approved   ☐ Disapproved _____   5/23/94
                                                      President   Date

Follow-up Action by Dean for Academic Services

1. Salary level and rank confirmed by _____   Eligible for Annuity Program _____
2. Pretenure review __1995-96__   Consideration by University Tenure Committee __1996-97__
3. Contract mailed _____   Contract returned _____
4. Remarks: _____

FACULTY PROSPECT INTERVIEW

Ref. AFP No. _____

Department/School Making Request: _____

Position No. _____   Position Title _____ ... FTE ____1____

Candidate's Name _____
      Last   First   M.   Social Security No

Degree Status: Ph.D.   Resume Attached: _X_ Yes ____ No   Recommendations Attached: _X_ Yes ____

Religious Commitment: Methodist

SUMMARY OF INTERVIEW

To Be Completed by the Vice President and COO for Academic Affairs

Interviewed by. *Dean Cooper, D Schmeltekof*   Date: *98*

Religious Commitment:

Methodist

Comments:

grew up in the Presbyterian denomination, becoming a Methodist upon his marriage to his Methodist wife. is an active Churchman, along with his family. He spoke convincingly about his Christian faith and his commitment to the values and aspirations of a Christian university.

Appendix 6

FACULTY PROSPECT INTERVIEW
Religious Affiliation

Ref. FPAF or FTPBA No. _____

Department/School Making Request: _____

Position No. _____   Position Title _____

Candidate's Name _____
            Last   First   M.   Social Security No.

To Be Completed by the Dean or Department Chair

Denominational affiliation/religious preference_____

Present church, parish, or synagogue involvement (including information about the candidate's participation and other points of clarification)

_____   _____
Dean or Department Chair   Date

SUMMARY OF INTERVIEW

To Be Completed by the Provost and Vice President for Academic Affairs

Interviewed by: _____   Date: _____

Comments:

_____   _____
Provost and Vice President for Academic Affairs   Date

Appendix 7

Dear Prospective Faculty Member of Baylor University:

We are pleased that you have indicated interest in teaching at Baylor University. We are the oldest institution of higher learning in the state of Texas—we were chartered by the Republic of Texas in 1845—and we are one of the half-dozen oldest institutions of higher learning west of the Mississippi River. Our heritage and our identity is that of a Baptist institution, founded for the purpose of providing a distinctively Christian education for various constituencies in Texas. Today, of course, our constituencies and our field of vision have broadened far beyond the state of Texas, but our world view remains unapologetically Christian.

Baylor University is a particular kind of institution. Intellectual trends of recent years have served to remind us all of the perspectival dimensions of human experience and the processes of learning. Indeed, it seems more obvious in the current intellectual climate — and certainly may be acknowledged as true without collapsing to some of the overly subjective trends of postmodernity — that institutions no less than people exhibit a certain particularity, a history and identity which give them a characteristic perspective from which they relate to the world of experience. Institutions of higher learning are no exception. There is no such thing as a university which is devoid of perspective. Baylor University was founded by Baptists for the express purpose of offering higher education on behalf of the Church and the (then) Republic of Texas from a general constellation of assumptions which were distinctively Christian.

It is because of these historic commitments that Baylor University has a unique opportunity in the public forum of ideas and within the broad landscape of higher education. Our varied constituencies deserve and we in good faith attempt to provide an education grounded in the great traditions of the liberal arts, energized by the commitment to service inherent in our faith, informed by the great ideas of ancient and modern thought, and enabled by the latest advances in scholarship and technology.

Thus, we who choose to serve at Baylor University face a different and perhaps more difficult task than do our colleagues at other kinds of institutions. We are committed to providing *Christian* higher education. To be sure, determining exactly what the phrase "Christian higher education" implies has proved a formidable task, a task which requires the continuous exploration of the relationship between faith and the academic enterprise, a task as ancient as the project of the second century AD Christian apologists who sought to integrate the faith of the crucified and risen Lord with the insights of their Greek philosophical traditions, and as contemporary as the recent "faith and learning" dialogues funded by the Lilly Foundation.

Though we continue to explore what it means to be an institution committed to Christian higher education, at Baylor we also endeavor to engage in this enterprise in a variety of specific ways. It seems to me that one of the most important ways is through the faculty. Undoubtedly, the Christian character of Baylor University is largely shaped by our faculty: the spiritual values of the faculty individually and collectively, the discipline with which faculty members pursue their academic work, the way students are treated both within and outside the classroom, the shape of the curriculum as constantly tested and modified by the faculty, and the intellectual content of the faculty's varied interactions with students. All of these tasks and responsibilities, carried largely by our faculty, are at the heart of Baylor's University's distinctiveness as an institution of Christian higher education.

Thus, Baylor University can remain true to its heritage only by recruiting, hiring, and developing faculty members who are committed as academic professionals to all the rigors of higher education as pursued through the common means of teaching, artistic creativity and performance, and research, while also being individuals who sincerely espouse and seek to express their academic and professional identities through the particularity of the Christian faith -- i.e., commitment to the universal lordship of the crucified and risen Jesus Christ.

We hope you will take seriously our interest in you, and we hope you will take seriously the importance of your genuine and sincere involvement in this great project of Christian higher education, should you come to Baylor. We seek neither a mindless faith nor religious indifference. We believe that the total person must be educated, and that as long as human beings are in some way essentially religious, there remains a legitimate role for institutions such as Baylor University. Our task would be easier if we chose either to bracket the Christian faith from the rigors of academic pursuits or to isolate our commitments as academicians from the great questions of meaning, value, and transcendence; but we choose to do neither. We believe that our mission as an institution of Christian higher education demands both the unfettered pursuit of all the truths of creation and also a thoughtful attempt to understand those hard won truths within a world view which finds its consummation in Jesus Christ.

Please do not hesitate to ask me or any member of our faculty or staff anything about the university or about what it could mean for you to work here with us and among us. We want you to continue to learn about us as you consider whether your participation in our community of learning and scholarship might be the appropriate means for achieving your own personal and professional goals, while at the same time furthering the mission and purpose of Baylor University. All the very best to you and yours.

Sincerely,

Robert B. Sloan, Jr.
President

1998

Appendix 8

MEMORANDUM

May 6, 1996

To: All Faculty

From: Donald D. Schmeltekopf, Provost and Vice President for Academic
         Affairs
         Kathy R. Hillman, Chair, Faculty Senate
         Daniel B. McGee, Chair, Faculty Committee on Academic Freedom,
         Responsibility, and Environment

Subject: Faculty Search Procedures

The attached "Faculty Search Procedures," "Baylor University in Perspective,"
and "Faculty Prospect Interview" have been approved by President Sloan upon the
recommendation of the Faculty Senate working through the Faculty Committee
on Academic Freedom, Responsibility, and Environment; the Council of Deans;
and the Provost.

We believe that the documents accurately express Baylor's mission, "to educate
men and women for worldwide leadership and service by integrating academic
excellence and Christian commitment within a caring community." We
appreciate the openness of the President and all others to varying points of view
on the issues involved and the hours of thought and discussion which have
contributed to the adoption of the policy aimed toward hiring outstanding faculty
members.

Thank you.

xc: President Robert B. Sloan, Jr.
       Vice Presidents
       Academic Deans

Faculty Search Procedures*

1. The department/school will include the following statement in advertisements for positions to be filled:

    "Baylor is a Baptist university affiliated with the Baptist General Convention of Texas. As an Affirmative Action/Equal Employment Opportunity Employer, Baylor encourages minorities, women, veterans, and persons with disabilities to apply."

2. When the department/school identifies from among the applicants those individuals who are candidates for a visit to campus, the dean or chairperson will send those candidates the following items:

    a. A copy of the Baylor University mission statement;

    b. A copy of "Baylor University in Perspective" (see attached);

    c. Any other information which the school or department advertising the position deems appropriate, such as a catalog, Baylor University "Fall Facts," and the faculty handbook**;

    d. A letter from the President.

3. Before inviting a candidate to campus for an interview, the dean or chairperson will ask the candidate to provide a statement of one to two pages describing his or her academic, professional, and personal goals and explaining how the pursuit of those goals will contribute to furthering Baylor University's mission. The department/school may also ask the candidate to provide written responses to additional inquiries concerning the candidate's suitability for the position for which he or she is being considered. (If a department/school wishes to elicit this same information in some other manner, for example through an interview at a professional meeting or by telephone, the department/school may do so at its discretion; however, a written report of this information must be added to the candidate's file before the department/school invites the candidate to campus.)

4. When candidates are interviewed at the departmental, school, and university levels, officials of the University will assure that the interview includes a discussion of both the academic and the Christian dimensions of Baylor University's mission and an exploration of how the candidate can contribute to furthering that mission.

5. Before the department/school can make an offer to a candidate, the "Faculty Prospect Interview" form on religious affiliation must be completed and made a part of the candidate's file (see attached).

*The recommendations contained in this document address particular procedures in the faculty search process and should not be interpreted as an exclusive description of all the policies and procedures involved in faculty searches.

**The Baylor University Faculty Handbook is scheduled for completion in the fall of 1996. When the handbook becomes available, candidates who are invited to campus for an interview will be provided a copy of the handbook.

Approved, May 1996, Baylor University

Chapter 8

An Alternative Vision for Baylor

Robert M. Baird

It would not be fitting at my age to toy with words, said Socrates at his trial. I am hardly Socrates, and I am not on trial (I don't think), but I am moving toward the age of Socrates when he was tried, so it would not be fitting for me either to toy with words. I shall try to be as direct and as persuasive as I can be.

Speaking of toying with words, let me say that one of the reasons I appreciate Don Schmeltekopf is that with him I have not had to toy with words. From the beginning of his tenure here our relationship has been open and honest. Don probably does not recall this, but several years ago, he and I were together and a third party introduced us to a fourth. Don was introduced as the provost and I as a faculty member. The person to whom we were introduced smiled and said to me, "I suppose you are properly deferential to your provost." Don got me off the hook. He smiled back and said, "That is not exactly how I would describe our relationship."

I hope that I have always been respectful to my provost, but rather than deferential I would describe my relationship with Don as collegial—a concept my mentor Jack Kilgore taught me to value highly. So let me say publicly how much I have appreciated my collegial relationship with Don over the years, a relationship that always included the invitation to express myself straightforwardly, especially when I disagreed with him. So, Don, congratulations to you on this occasion, and to honor our relationship, I will continue not to toy with words.

Could we pursue an issue more important than the hiring, promotion, and tenure policies of Baylor University? We are discussing the future of Baylor, the kind of Baylor we want to become.

Baylor 2012 has two major trajectories: increased emphasis on research and publication and a different approach to securing the religious identity of the university. These trajectories are reflected in the current hiring policy, which differs from the past by focusing on the candidate's potential for research and publication and by more explicitly examining the candidate's religious life. I want to make a brief comment about the first trajectory and then focus on the second.

The First Trajectory: Research and Publication

The first trajectory raises two questions that as a community we must continually address. Will we hire sufficient faculty to reduce teaching responsibilities so that publication expectations of the faculty can be met? Will we continue to value teaching and nurturing students, so that neither teaching nor students get lost in the shuffle? The question of hiring more faculty is a matter of resources. This is simply a problem. It is not a simple problem, but it is simply a problem; by that, I mean that finding the resources could solve it.

The second question, the question of honoring teaching and the nurturing of students in the face of publication requirements, is a different matter. That is a dilemma to be continually coped with, not a problem to be solved. The dilemma arises not because of any incompatibility between research and high quality teaching. To the contrary, high quality teaching presupposes disciplined study and research. The dilemma arises because of the publication expectations. Once publication in top tier journals is required for tenure, young faculty focused on earning tenure can feel pressure to put class preparation and involvement with students on the "back burner." To counter this possibility, we will have to be intentional in our on-going emphasis on high quality teaching and devotion to students. Balancing the demands of research and the nurturing of students is a challenge, and this challenge is a dilemma precisely because this balancing act will always be with us—we don't solve it, we learn how creatively to cope with it. This is a matter of institutional and individual faculty will.

The Second Trajectory: Religious Identity

The focus of this paper, however, is the second trajectory of the new vision: the current approach to the religious identity of the university, which involves a more explicit and detailed examination of the candidate's religious life.

When faculty search committees begin their tasks, they are given a set of criteria by the administration to guide the undertaking. Prominently in first place is a criterion that emphasizes this increased focus on the religious life of the prospective candidate. It reads, "The successful candidate will be vigorous in the life of faith, easily at home with [the] Christian confession and thus warmly committed to the fellowship and work of the church."[1] In passing let me say that I have been associated with Baylor in one way or another since my student days in the mid to late 1950s. In my experience, Baylor faculty by-and-large have always been "vigorous in the life of faith, easily at home with [the] Christian confession and . . . warmly committed to the fellowship and work of the church." When I was an undergraduate at Baylor many of the people I encountered at church on Sunday were teachers I encountered at Baylor on Monday. My Sunday school teacher was my history professor, Ralph Lynn.

The religious identity of the university has been secure in the past, is now secure, and I see no evidence that its ongoing security needs a more rigorous examination of the religious commitments of prospective faculty. Moreover, this intense emphasis on the religious criterion for Baylor faculty may prevent us from hiring men and women who could contribute significantly to Baylor's intellectual and spiritual life.

Vignette One: Haywood Shuford

Let me, then, advance a slightly altered vision for Baylor. I will begin with three biographical vignettes, the purpose of which, I hope, will become clear. When I transferred to Baylor as a sophomore in 1956, my life was transformed because of my teachers. One of the most remarkable was Haywood Shuford. From Brown University, Shuford was on this faculty only ten years, but his influence on a decade of philosophy students was monumental. Anyone familiar with the department during those days knows what a demanding, exciting, and fertile place it was. Shuford was the catalyst. We flocked around him like Socratic disciples, despite our gut-wrenching fear that he would catch us out in what he called "logical howlers."

In a recent issue of the *Collegium*, published by our College of Arts and Sciences, several alumni were asked to reflect on their undergraduate life at Baylor. One was David Solomon, professor of philosophy at Notre Dame and the keynote speaker at this colloquium. Thinking about his days at Baylor, David says at one point, "Ann Miller and Clement Goode, Ralph Lynn and Bob Reid were our mentors and idols, but for me philosophy was at the heart of things." Solomon then talks about Haywood Shuford, from whom he took eight courses. Of Shuford Solomon says, he "changed my life as surely and as radically as if he had taken off the top of my skull and stirred my brains with a soup spoon."[2] Shuford did the same for me, for Carl Vaught, for Stuart Rosenbaum, for Dallas Willard, and many others.

What makes Shuford's influence even more remarkable is that most of us eventually rejected his way of doing philosophy, but he himself, the disciplined way he worked, the seriousness with which he took the life of the mind, his commitment to thinking clearly got into our souls, into our blood.

The year after I completed my M.A. degree, the philosophy department had a one-year opening and I remained for a year as an instructor. I came to know Shuford from the perspective of a young colleague. He was not vigorous in the life of faith in any traditionally recognizable sense. He was not a churchman. To tell you the truth, I am not sure what his religious views were. I do know that religion was a difficult matter for him. Difficult, I suspect, because he needed more evidence or evidence of a different kind than the religious life permits. But he played a powerful role, indeed a spiritual role, in my life, awakening me from my dogmatic slumbers. To honor him, I must not toy with words. I do not think that Shuford could be hired at Baylor today, but my dream is of a Baylor that makes room for the Haywood Shufords of the world.

Vignette Two: Charles Hartshorne

Students of philosophy are often moved by the written words of great thinkers. The dialogues of Plato inspire many. My colleague Carl Vaught spent a sabbatical in Nova Scotia, often sitting by the water's edge, reading Augustine's *Confessions* aloud. Stuart Rosenbaum will come to my office eager to read me a passage from

John Dewey. Though the passage might seem downright opaque to me, normally understated Stuart is beside himself with enthusiasm. And I recall how moved I was when I first read Charles Hartshorne's book *Divine Relativity*.

A graduate of Harvard University, Hartshorne taught at the University of Chicago, Emory University, and the University of Texas. He died two years ago at the age of 103. My last personal memory of him was an early morning walk the two of us took at a conference we were attending. The walk was brisk. He set the pace. He was 91 years old.

Hartshorne was in a talkative mood that morning. And most of the talk was about God and Hartshorne's belief that a clear-headed understanding of God was essential to a coherent and comprehensive philosophical view.   God-intoxicated, he helped many a young philosopher learn to love God with all of his or her mind.

The article on Hartshorne in the Stanford Encyclopedia of Philosophy emphasizes that he is considered by many to be "one of the most important philosophers of religion and metaphysicians of the twentieth century."[3]   The highly regarded contemporary process thinker, John Cobb, calls Hartshorne "the Einstein of religious thought."[4]

Arguably, Charles Hartshorne took the reality of and the nature of God as seriously as any thinker who ever lived. And he was open about his own commitments. In the preface to *Divine Relativity*, he says: "I do not conceal my own faith . . . that theistic religion . . . reformulated. . . is true . . . ."[5] But his mind and his integrity required that he reformulate classical theism, and he had difficulty with the doctrine of the trinity. His closest religious identification was with the Unitarian Church.

To honor a man I casually knew, but admired from afar, I must not toy with words. I do not think he could be hired at Baylor. Our articulated hiring policy excludes Unitarians. My dream is of a Baylor that makes room for the Charles Hartshornes of the world.

Vignette Three: Michael Ruse

In the spring of 2002, the Herbert H. Reynolds Lecturer was Dr. Michael Ruse, holder of a chair in philosophy at Florida State University. Ruse is the author, at my last count, of eighteen books published by such presses as Harvard, Cambridge, Oxford, and the University of Chicago. When Harvard Press received the last manuscript of Harvard's own paleontologist Stephen Gould, the only person in the country to whom they sent even part of the manuscript for evaluation was Michael Ruse,[6] a testimony to his reputation in the academy.

Having returned home after his two weeks on the Baylor campus, Ruse wrote the following to my colleague, James Marcum. "When, three years ago, I was asked to accept the Reynolds Lectureship, I confess that I did not know much about Baylor University. I knew that it was private, in Texas, and affiliated with the Baptists. But I knew little more. Now, having spent two weeks on the campus, and having met many people associated with Baylor . . . I . . . know much more about the institution, its history, its ideals, its accomplishments and its hopes for the future. In these rather dark days, when so many in the world dislike and criticize the things for which America stands [this was post nine-eleven], it is good for those of us who are not Americans (I was born in England, and, before moving South to Florida, lived and taught for forty years in Canada) to remember that there are some things that the United States does very well indeed . . . [for example], its top-quality institutions of higher education, of which Baylor is one."

Ruse continued, "I was impressed beyond measure by the standards that are set and achieved at Baylor. . . . Even more was I impressed by the integrity of everyone . . . . Baylor's Christian ethos of a vital kind is there for everyone to see—even [by] those who do not share the Baptist faith, even [by] those like [me] who have no faith at all. It is hardly too much to say that everyone is bound by cords of love and respect: for teachers, for students, and for support staff. For me, spending time at Baylor was a privilege, for which I am grateful and humbled." Ruse concluded his letter with the statement that he feels passionate about his subject, "not so much for the content but because I think great ideas are truly exciting, and the ability to respond to them is much of the real meaning of being made in the image of the Creator."[7]

Though he describes himself as one who does not experience personal faith, everything I know of Michael Ruse indicates that he cherishes his own Quaker heritage and respects the life of faith; indeed, in the public forum he often challenges those who do not respect the life of faith. What an addition he would make to the intellectual conversation of this community! On the day of his Reynolds Lecture, more people were turned away at the door who wanted to hear him than were sitting and standing in the "crammed" auditorium. But again, not to toy with words, our hiring policy would exclude him. My dream is of a Baylor that makes room for the Michael Ruses of the world.

An Altered Vision for Baylor

I have included some detail in these vignettes, for implicit in them is an argument for a certain kind of Baylor. Let me conclude by briefly fleshing out that argument.

By its very nature a religiously affiliated intellectual community lives with tension. To be religiously affiliated is to be part of a tradition with certain substantive values and to be committed to deepening and transmitting those values. But to be an intellectual community is also to pursue inquiry wherever that inquiry leads and to stimulate students to think independently, to think in new and creative ways. But that is a risky venture, for the intellectual inquiry and the provoking of students may lead, at times, in directions at odds with dimensions of the religious tradition of the institution. Confronted with this risk, one option is to sacrifice the religious heritage; another is to restrict the intellectual inquiry. To take the road less traveled, to sacrifice neither spiritual heritage nor open inquiry is Baylor's risky path. It is a path that will involve continuing debate about where we draw the line so that we preserve both our religious identity and a stimulating intellectual life. The issue is dramatically faced in our hiring and promotion policy. I recommend that we draw the line to include the Shufords, the Hartshornes, and the Ruses of the world. I recommend that we draw the line in such a way that when Baylor has an opening in World Religions or Asian History or Comparative Philosophy we be open to the possibility of a Muslim or a Buddhist or a Hindu.

At this point, let me acknowledge that I appreciate the concern that many at Baylor have over the demise of religiously affiliated colleges and universities in the United States, an unfortunate demise for it lessens the diversity in American higher education. I also appreciate the claim that without an intentional commitment to our religious heritage such a demise could happen right here in "River City," that is to say, in Waco, that is to say, at Baylor. I do appreciate that concern.

So my vision of Baylor is a vision of an institution proud of its Christian heritage and deeply committed to sustaining its Christian tradition. But my dream is also of a Baylor so secure in its identity that it willingly embraces some faculty who are not full embodiments of that heritage and tradition.

Why? Because it would make for a more vibrant intellectual community, because it would indicate our desire to converse with and to learn from other voices, and because it would dramatically symbolize our confidence as a Christian community.

In a recent article in the *Baylor Line*, our provost was quoted as articulating the university's scholarly aspirations by his "blunt statement that 'Baylor should act and feel like Notre Dame.'"[8] His point was that "'Notre Dame is a vibrant, intellectual place.'"[9] Indeed, Notre Dame is one of the leading intellectual communities in this country. Moreover, there is no institution of higher education more closely identified with its religious heritage than Notre Dame is with its Catholicism. The two, intellectual prominence and religious identity, can certainly coexist.

I recently received a print-out of the various religious affiliations of the Notre Dame faculty. Notre Dame hires Muslims. Further, the provost at Notre Dame, Nathan Hatch, was quoted in the same recent issue of the *Baylor Line* as indicating that "there is no specific requirement to belong to a church at Notre Dame."[10] In hiring new faculty, Hatch says, "the typical thing is to describe the Notre Dame culture and then ask candidates what they think of it and how they would fit in."[11] He emphasizes that with regard to tenure decisions, the religious commitments of faculty are not scrutinized. He adds, "We have never felt comfortable weighing someone's spirituality."[12] Let me note lest I be accused of not presenting the full picture of Nathan Hatch, he is also quoted in the *Line* as saying that "Baylor has undertaken a marvelous experiment and a wonderful challenge. I'm delighted that Baylor has set its course to do that."[13] But the point is that Notre Dame with a more open hiring policy has achieved what Baylor wants to achieve. My dream is that in this regard, we do what the provost recommends: let's emulate Notre Dame.

Some Christians have advanced an interesting criticism of secular institutions that goes like this: Young candidates interviewing for jobs at secular universities discover that if they are Marxists, or feminists, or gay liberationists, that hardly raises an eyebrow, but if they are openly Christian, that raises more than eyebrows, that raises a barrier to employment. Christians, the argument goes, are often advised by their mentors not to let their religious identity out on the table if they want to be a viable candidate for a position in a secular university. I do not know how true this claim is. If and to whatever extent it is true, shame on secular higher education, for it is an expression of intellectual closed-mindedness, and that is a betrayal of the essence of an intellectual community.

Let us be a model of openness by inviting to our faculty other voices. I know! This is a complicated issue; I do not want to appear naive. If Baylor is going to retain its Christian identity, she must hire and retain a large majority of faculty members who confessionally identify with this tradition. In that sense the religious issue must always be on the table in the hiring process. But that is compatible with a more open hiring policy.

My dream is of a hiring and tenuring process which would publicly assert the following three principles. First, by heritage and ongoing commitment we are Christians with a Baptist heritage; to support that commitment, other matters being equal, we will give preference in hiring to those who reflect this heritage in their own religious pilgrimage. Second, while as an institution we do not expect every faculty member to be professionally involved in a disciplinary integration of faith and learning, we want to provide leadership in this area of academic life; to that end, we will provide unique opportunities for those who have these research and publication interests. Third, we are open to hiring individuals from diverse religious backgrounds and even those for whom religious commitment is a struggle, as long as they understand the Christian mission of the university and as long as they believe that they can live out their professional lives constructively and enthusiastically in such a community.

My wife, Alice, and I are in the grandparent phase of life. It is highly unlikely that our granddaughter Lia or our grandson Malcolm will come to Baylor. Lia will likely grow up in California and Malcolm in Michigan. I would love it if they came here, of course. And make no mistake about it. If they did, I would want them to encounter Robert Sloan, and Don Schmeltekopf, and David Jeffrey, and Ralph Wood, and Steve Evans, and Mike Beaty, and all those whose names are associated closely with the religious vision of Baylor 2012. But my dream, informed by my head and my heart, is of a Baylor where they could also encounter and have ongoing relationships with the Haywood Shufords, the Charles Hartshornes, and the Michael Ruses of the world. And who knows, perhaps also a Muslim or a Buddhist or a Hindu. Such a Baylor would symbolize a confident engagement with God's diverse world. That is my dream, my vision of Baylor 2012.

Notes

[1] Provost and Deans of various colleges and schools, memo to Department Chairs and Search Committees, Baylor University, Texas, 12 Oct. 2001.

[2] "Alumni in Academia," *Collegium* 2002: 21.

[3] Dan Dombrowski, "Charles Hartshorne," *The Stanford Encyclopedia of Philosophy*, ed. Edward N. Zatta, Fall 2001 <http://plato.stanford.edu/archives/fall2001/entries/hartshorne/>.

[4] John Cobb, "Charles Hartshorne: The Einstein of Religious Thought," The Center for Process Studies, Claremont, California, 8 Feb. 2003 <http://www.ctr4process.org>.

[5] Charles Hartshorne, *The Divine Relativity: A Social Conception of God* (New Haven: Yale University Press, 1948) xi.

[6] Richard Monastersky, "Revising the Book of Life," *The Chronicle of Higher Education*, 15 Mar. 2002.

[7] Michael Ruse, e-mail to James Marcum, 12 July 2002. Permission to quote obtained from Ruse.

[8] Meg Cullar, "Creating the Faculty of the Future," *Baylor Line*, Winter 2003: 38.

[9] Cullar 38.

[10] Cullar 43.

[11] Cullar 43.

[12] Cullar 43.

[13] Cullar 43.

Chapter 9

Emphasizing "Community" in a Community of Scholars

Diana R. Garland

I am rather uniquely qualified to respond to this conversation, having been relieved of my appointment as dean in another Baptist institution because I questioned the hiring policies of the administration. That institution had so narrowly defined its understanding of acceptable religiosity that I could not find qualified faculty candidates. Because of that experience, I remain rather sensitive about the ways we define criteria for hiring and promotion, as you might imagine. It is evidence of the academic environment open to rigorous dialogue that Don Schmeltekopf has helped to create that I am willing to comment on this topic.

A major concept of Christianity is that we are joined in Christ to one another, that we need one another, and that we are to live in community. We are known to be Jesus' disciples, Jesus said, by how we love one another.[1] What can this mean to us as a university that seeks to be known foremost as Christian in character? Perhaps one of the most significant contributions Baylor University can make to academia and to scholarship is to become a living critique of the dangers of American individualism as it plays itself out in the academy. If we choose to risk such a critique, we can become a model of a Christian academic *community*. To be Christian does not refer simply to our individual acceptance of a checklist of distinctive beliefs but, rather, to the ways we live out those beliefs in our life together. What might that mean in thinking about hiring and promotion? What if we *helped one another* get over the bar that Mikeal Parsons talked about, helped one another in intentional, institutionalized ways? In fact, perhaps individual high jumping is not the sports metaphor we need at all. The metaphor of a *team* sport, where success is about the individual's performance in concert with the whole group, could inspire the vision of the major academic contribution Baylor can make. We can do this in several ways:

Evaluating individuals in their community context: We could become the community Stephen Evans described, where conversation about grand narratives and our connection to them is part of the warp and woof of our life together, in a place where those narratives are lived out as colleagues, partnering and collaborating with one another. The elements are already here, if we don't lose them in new structures of scholarly expectations that emphasize the individual and only tolerate corporate academic products. When I came to Baylor five years ago, I remember vividly those first months when I was trying to figure out how to do what I was brought here to do, which was to develop a new graduate program. I experienced support and willingness to collaborate everywhere I turned on this campus. Faculty and staff in my own department and across the campus taught me about Waco and Texas and Texas Baptists. They helped me learn to navigate the complexity of the explicit policies of the university but also explained the real ways things are done and pointed out where the landmines are. They helped me deal with the shock of pulling up deep roots and moving to a new community in midlife. Not many academic environments can be so described.

However, we need to take this community a step further. What if we valued collaboration not only as evidence of *collegiality* but also as vital to *scholarship* in this place? We might recognize that faculty members' contributions not only *may,* but *should* complement one another. Chairs and deans would be evaluated on the extent to which they build academic teams and productive communities of scholarship. For example, in the professional disciplines, one who excels in community service might, in the process of serving, explore and expand an approach to professional practice, which then might become the subject of academic study and publication by a colleague. Should we not value that kind of partnership in our tenure and promotion decisions?

Providing safety for taking risks: We can become a community that embodies grace, so that all of us feel safe to risk, knowing that sometimes people fail. We can pursue what it means to be Christians and scholars not only in our experiments and publications but also in the way we structure our lives together and relate to one another.

Robert Baird's comments about his relationship over the years with Donald Schmeltekopf speak to that kind of living grace, the freedom to speak our minds and hearts to one another. Someone has said that if you haven't failed lately, then you haven't been taking enough risks. We need the safety to try grand experiments that flop as well as to fail in all the small ways that happen when people are working hard and plowing creative new ground together, safety to risk not only in what we are researching but also in how we do that research in community with one another.

Including the whole community: We can recognize overtly, in tangible ways, that our scholarship is a product of a community of colleagues, administrators, secretaries, maintenance staff, cleaning personnel, and board members. How is Christianity reflected in how we pay administrators and lecturers and secretaries, in how we relate to the physical environment and the social communities where we find ourselves planted? How do we enfold lecturers and part-time faculty in the pursuit of our mission, and recognize and nurture their contribution? It is not just that we act "Christianly" to everyone, but that we recognize the *necessity* of all those in this place to the success of what we as individuals are tempted to take credit for as our products alone.

Distinguishing between criteria for hiring and criteria for tenure: Parsons' concern is on target; many promising candidates for our faculty, prior to entertaining the option of coming to Baylor, have not had an opportunity for and may even have been strongly discouraged from reflecting on the integration of their faith with their teaching and research. I am concerned about the potential great thinkers and researchers who may be excluded before we have a chance to embrace them in a community that can call out and develop those gifts. It has indeed been my experience, as Baird has noted, that faculty candidates in many social work programs in other institutions, both public and private, even religiously affiliated, would sink their candidacies by mentioning that they are interested in integrating religious faith with their scholarship. Perhaps, then, we must recognize that the hiring process must be one of risk, bringing people into our community who feel called to our mission and appear to have the potential and commitment to living it with us, but who may not yet have much to show for that calling. If we are willing to take these risks in hiring, we must then recognize that this integration takes time and needs to be nurtured in a community of scholars in conversation and collaboration with one another. We are not only in the process of *finding* world class Christian scholars; we should also be *growing* them.

Making service to the community and world outside *the Baylor bubble central as evidence of valuable scholarship:* Baird raises the dilemma of balancing the demands of research and teaching. I want to add to that the demands of service to community and world. Evans described the Anabaptist emphasis on radical discipleship, the view that thinking is reshaped by living in a distinctive way. To take a secular model, service-learning is not just applicable to students but to the whole academic community, especially to how we think about our scholarship. If Waco, Texas, is not a better place, better environmentally, economically, and socially by the year 2012, then I wonder if we have really embraced what it means to be a Christian university. Should not the integration of faith with our disciplines be evidenced in improving the teaching in the Waco public elementary and secondary schools, cleaning up the water, lowering the poverty rate, reducing family violence, creating a city known for its artistic beauty, and improving race relations? Does not all our research have practical implications, and doesn't being Christian mean that we live those implications? If we want to be a premier *Christian* university, our faculty promotion policies should address not only research and teaching, but also how faculty members are making a difference in the community around us, whether locally or globally or something in between. Further, however, it is not just that we are called to serve, but that service is essential in shaping and informing our uniquely Christian contribution to the grand tasks of academic inquiry.

Notes

---

[1] John 13: 35

Chapter 10

Unashamed and Unafraid

Mark Osler

To oversimplify what Drs. Baird and Parsons have set out, I would represent the hiring practices at Baylor several years ago with two simple categories: (1) Churchgoers and (2) the Uncommitted. Baird seems to be saying that we lose something by rejecting those who fall into the second category, that many of those who are not churchgoers (or who go to churches inconsistent with our beliefs) not only could be wonderful teachers, but could also stimulate our thought on matters of faith. In contrast, Parsons urges us to concentrate on the first category, but to focus on moving it upward to something beyond church attendance. He further acknowledges that under Dr. Schmeltekopf, this has already happened.

In short, my response to their proposals is that we add a third category. This new category would encompass an unusual and important group: those scholars and teachers who are so unashamed of their Christian faith that they are unafraid to take their resulting scholarship to the larger secular academy.

Not every hire would be in this category, but if we can attract and keep such scholars and teachers, they will be the ones who define us to the larger world and to our students. In general, it is fair to say that Christian universities have been unashamed of their faith, but that it has been the great secular universities who have been unafraid of the often contentious, even anarchic world of scholarly work and criticism. If we are to be a great Christian university, it is being unashamed of our faith that will mark us as Christian and being unafraid of the larger academy that will mark us as a great university. It is being *both* unashamed and unafraid that will mark us as unique.

What do I mean when I refer to those who are unashamed and unafraid? I do not simply mean those who call themselves Christian, but those whose Christianity suffuses their lives in a whole and challenging way. For many of these Christians, their faith life will be marked not by comfort, but by struggle, as the teachings of Christ often clash with the majority view. Christian ideas about wealth, about forgiveness, and about charity often clash with the accepted views in many of our fields. In my own field, criminal law, the Christian practitioner must struggle with the imperatives of Christ. For the defense attorney, the troubling question is how justice informs the work of defending those accused of crime, while for the prosecutor the problem is how to reconcile the idea of mercy with the everyday work of enforcing secular laws.

And what do I mean when I describe them as unafraid? As I use that phrase, I mean they are scholars who are willing to look beyond the walls of our institution and the family of Christian universities to have their ideas challenged in the larger public forum. In so doing, they expose themselves to the possible criticism that Christianity is archaic, and they must respond to such criticism with grace and wisdom.

If we have at the heart of our community those who are unashamed and unafraid, we will be able to address two serious concerns, one more often discussed than the other. The first, which we hear in reaction to Baird's proposals, is that if we allow those we consider insufficiently committed to Christianity to be a part of Baylor, that "bottom rung" will eventually overwhelm our identity and we will become secular. The second more subtle danger is that if we instead focus on the first group, churchgoers (even while excluding the second group), we may lose our identity nonetheless because those we have chosen live an easy faith of accommodation, which erects no barriers and burns no hearts. It would be better, in fact, for us to have some from each of the three groups I have described than a faculty made up entirely of those whose faith is only an identity, not a passion.

I don't want Baylor to become secular. I am a graduate of Yale, and I loved my time there. At Yale I learned to be a scholar and to love the law. Deeply engrained in me, though, is the memory of walking through that beautiful campus on a fall afternoon, the maple trees ablaze.

Looking up as I walked through the heart of campus, past the Sterling Library, I could see what look like cathedrals and chapels, with crosses and angels in the architecture. But now they have all become ghosts. Long ago, Jonathan Edwards left those buildings, leaving us students as sinners in the hands of no God at all.

The table of the academy is a large one. When the spirit of the Puritan Jonathan Edwards left Yale, a seat at that table became vacant. If we choose as faculty members those who are unashamed and unafraid to become the heart of this university, that empty chair can become our place at the table.

Chapter 11

Hiring, Tenure, and Promotion in the "New" Baylor

Charles A. Weaver, III

At the outset, let me add my voice to those offering Don Schmeltekopf heartfelt thanks and appreciation for his distinguished service as Provost of Baylor University. Though my time at Baylor predates Don's by a year or two, in most significant ways our careers at Baylor have completely intertwined. During the past two years, in my role with the Faculty Senate, I have met with Don on a regular basis, discussing a variety of issues. Though we have not always initially agreed on actions or outcomes, most of the time we eventually did. I can state without reservation that we always proceeded with an air of mutual respect, good faith, and a recognition that our ultimate goals were similar. When the Faculty Senate recently honored Don at our March meeting, we presented him with a plaque engraved with the signatures of all chairs of the Senate with whom Don has worked. Without exception, these past chairs welcomed the opportunity to express their appreciation.

During the early stages of planning for this Colloquy, someone asked who would be giving the "official Baylor position" on each issue. Don interrupted, absolutely insistent that no one would be giving the official position. He very bluntly stated that he was interested in the project only if participants felt free to espouse disparate opinions on these issues in free and open dialog. If there was not respectful controversy and disagreement, he said, it would not be worth doing. I took those instructions seriously.

I should add a disclaimer. I am one of the few speaking at this gathering who was chosen not because of my keen intellect and insights, but because of the role I occupy. I am currently the Chair of the Faculty Senate. I suggest you lower your expectations accordingly.

Having read the papers by Mikeal Parsons and Robert Baird, I find myself in the unusual position of agreeing with both of them, up to a point. I would suggest that Baylor has long-since adopted the "Significant Contribution Model" advocated by Parsons. What has changed during the past few years, however, is how we determine what constitutes a "significant contribution." First, the University clearly expects more from faculty in terms of scholarship and publication. During a recent interview with the *Waco Tribune-Herald*,[1] I was correctly quoted as saying that Baylor has become a "publish or perish" institution. This quote was not well received by some senior administrators. I was told that Baylor is not publish-or-perish, because that phrase conveys a single-minded pursuit of scholarly productivity at the expense of other aspects of the academic life (like teaching). Such a semantic distinction is likely one of small comfort to those who were denied tenure in the past few years, the vast majority terminated because they failed to publish in sufficient quantity.

The message new faculty members are hearing is clear: publish, and publish well. Does this mean that Baylor no longer values teaching? Not necessarily. Too often this discussion misses the point entirely. I have lost count of the number of times I have heard indignant rejections of the assertion that publication and teaching excellence are mutually exclusive. The problem with this indignation is that no one ever asserted that productive scholars were incapable teachers in the first place. This has become the "lie repeated often enough," unfortunately. What is beyond debate, however, is that an increased emphasis on publication must come at the expense of something, usually the amount of teaching. Newly hired Baylor faculty members simply don't teach as much as they once did.

Further, I do believe that Baylor tolerates mediocre teaching—competent, mind you, but not exceptional—to a much greater degree than it once did. As an institution, we have fairly well settled on the lower bounds of "acceptable" scholarly output. We have a number of faculty who have been denied tenure in the past five years because they did not publish enough. We are still exploring the lower bounds of teaching effectiveness.

The second significant change I have noticed in my nearly fifteen years at Baylor is the diminished, and diminishing, degree of interaction between faculty and undergraduate students. I spend much less time with students than I once did, but the most striking aspect of this is on the part of the student. I do not turn students away from my office, nor do I hide during office hours. Students simply do not come by as often. Rightly or wrongly, they have no expectation that faculty will be as accessible as they once were. Oddly, the current students don't mourn this change as a loss, as they have never known otherwise.

The third significant change during my time at Baylor, and in many ways the most disturbing trend, has nothing to do with publication or teaching excellence. As Baird says, the relative balance between teaching and research will always be a matter of discussion and accommodation. No, the most critical issue facing the university is exactly how we determine the other activities that make up one's "significant contribution" to the university community. The phrase that produces the greatest anxiety among faculty is the phrase "supportive of the mission of the university." As Parsons discusses, quantifying this part of a faculty member's performance is difficult, if not impossible. (I would disagree with his off-hand comment about "Tier One" churches. Of course there are Tier One churches in Waco, and every Baylor faculty member could list them.) But I submit that is exactly what Baylor is now doing at every stage of the hiring, retention, and promotion process.

As I see it, there are two intellectually defensible ways of implementing religious expectations of faculty. The first, what I'll refer to as the current Notre Dame model, is essentially what Baylor followed during the McCall and Reynolds administrations. When prospective faculty members were hired, they were expected to be in sympathy with the mission of Baylor. Once hired, though, faculty members were not again questioned about their religious beliefs and practices. At Notre Dame, in fact, according to Provost Nathan Hatch, the university is careful not to intrude into a faculty member's religious commitment. He said, "we've never felt comfortable weighing someone's spirituality."[2]

The second defensible way would be to list an explicit set of guidelines such as statements of faith, codes of faculty conduct, etc., which must be followed by faculty. I don't want to be at a university that has such practices, but there would be little room for discussion among faculty who are denied tenure on these grounds.

In contrast, Baylor's current model for evaluating religious commitments in hiring, tenure, and promotion is dangerously close to "discernment." We have expectations, but they are not articulated. We expect faculty to be "vigorous in the life of faith, easily at home with Christian confession, and thus warmly committed to the fellowship and work of the church." But how can faculty demonstrate that they are "vigorous" in their faith? Prospective faculty are sometimes turned away after brief administrative interviews when they are judged insufficiently "warm and reflective" in their beliefs. In reality, we are often passing judgment on one's capacity for spiritual growth and development.

Like Parsons, I admire Notre Dame's "significant contribution" model. More than that, however, I admire the security and openness with which they approach hiring, promotion, and tenure. They have no fear that the university will stray off course if they hire non-Catholics, or even non-Christians. They feel no need to evaluate rigorously the spiritual fitness of prospective faculty; indeed, the provost of the university rarely inserts himself into the interview process at all. Notre Dame displays a degree of trust and respect between faculty and administration that is commonplace at many institutions and has been a part of Baylor's past. It is unfortunate that we now find it enviable.

Evolutionary biologists have long recognized the concept of "hybrid vigor" in organisms. Members of a species who have diverse and complex backgrounds are more adaptable to changes in their environment and over the long run tend to be much more successful. More homogeneous groups, on the other hand, tend to become more narrowly defined over time. They may be able to exploit a small niche, perhaps, but they are less capable of adapting to even small changes in their environment. To extend this analogy, I fear that the current selective pressure at Baylor is creating a more uniform, homogenous faculty. Rather than producing world-class faculty capable of thriving at any academic institution, we are increasingly becoming a faculty adapted to a narrower concept of a "faith-based university." Ironically, by ensuring that every faculty member fits this narrow definition, we may be becoming a faculty less "fit" for Tier 1 status. Diversity and dissent should not be stifled; they should be encouraged, even celebrated.

I would hope those in a position to evaluate the depth of a faculty member's support of the mission recognize there will be different but acceptable ways of doing this. Some of us believe we are acting out our Christian call by supporting Planned Parenthood or the Sierra Club. When it comes to matters of faith, good people can honestly disagree. Jim Johnson, my pastor at First Presbyterian Church, often describes our congregation by saying, "we believe that if our hearts are one, our minds need not be."

As just one example, the Department of Religion continues to struggle in their search for a Baptist—the rules are ever tougher for the Department of Religion—who specializes in world religions. Would the university's mission be compromised if a Methodist were hired in that position? Further, some of the best candidates are likely to be non-Christian. Are we afraid that students being taught by an Islamic faculty member might convert from Christianity to Islam?

In conclusion, while I agree with Parsons' endorsement of the significant contribution model of Notre Dame, I find Baird's portrayal of a more open and confident Baylor to hold the most appeal. I am reasonably confident that this is not "misplaced nostalgia," as I'm not yet old enough to be nostalgic. Rather, I simply find an atmosphere of mutual trust and respect, one where faculty pursue both scholarly and spiritual questions out of attraction rather than fear, to be the true embodiment of a "world-class Christian University."

Notes

---

[1] J. Embry, "BU wants faculty with the write stuff," *The Waco Tribune-Herald*, 9 Feb. 2003, 1A, 8A.

[2] Meg Cullar, "Creating the Faculty of the Future," *Baylor Line*, Winter 2003: 43.

Part Three

*What Does It Mean to Support
the "Mission" of a Christian University?*

Chapter 12

The Convergence of Research and Institutional Mission: A Faculty Perspective

Owen Lind

[F]or so he saith expressly, 'The glory of God is to conceal a thing, but the glory of the king is to find it out': as if, according to the innocent play of children, the Divine Majesty took delight to hide his works, to the end to have them found out; and as if kings could not obtain a greater honour than to be God's play-fellows in that game.[1]
Francis Bacon

This colloquy—to honor Donald Schmeltekopf—is highly appropriate because the content provides a divergence of opinion regarding the character of Baylor University. Don surely appreciates and encourages the counter-opinion. We, as diverse and eccentric scholars, thank him for that. I particularly wish to thank Don for his "Vision" because without this vision, my paper would have no title—the convergence of which I will speak would have been quite different. My paper is in no way a Baylor history. Others, much more qualified, have already provided that. This is perception—the perception of scholarly expectations by a natural scientist over a thirty-seven-year career journey at Baylor and marked by a slow convergence of personal goals and the university's mission. One can only wonder, looking back, if today's new faculty can possibly be as naive regarding the working of academe in general and their chosen university in particular as was I in 1966. I have augmented my

125

perceptions of the changing scholarship expectations in the natural sciences with perceptions of several faculty members from other disciplines whose tenures also date to the 1960s. In the last portion I express opinions regarding Christian scholarship and suggest a possible direction for emphasis by Baylor's natural science and allied disciplines.

To enable one to support Baylor's mission, one must have a reasonable concept of that mission. How is our mission different from the mission of any other university? Is our mission dynamic and changing in part or in whole? At the fundamental level, I do not perceive that Baylor's mission has changed in the years of my tenure, but the interpretation of and the means for implementing the mission certainly have. Perhaps the essence of the mission is contained in the University motto: *Pro Ecclesia, Pro Texana.* As a scientist, I probably should not venture too far into the *ecclesia* part but leave that up to my colleague, Ralph Wood. (Nonetheless, I do venture there a bit because it is central to my science: i.e., faith and learning is not a program, but a way of life.) But *Pro Texana* provides an appropriate metaphor for the university's role in serving society—not only Texas but global society—through scholarship. Simply put, the mission of a university is to create and maintain a "community of scholars"—a community encompassing both the greenest freshman and the most accomplished Nobel Laureate. The task of this community is the discovery of knowledge and its transmission, not only to one another, but to society as well. Richard Feynman put this well when he asked,

> why is it possible for people to stay so woefully ignorant and yet reasonably happy in modern society when so much knowledge is unavailable to them? . . . I think we should teach them wonders and that the purpose of knowledge is to appreciate wonders even more. And that the knowledge is just to put into correct framework the wonder that nature is.[2]

This transmission of knowledge can be said to be the academic mission of every university, but Baylor's mission has always had an additional component: at Baylor those responsible for the transmission of knowledge compose a community of scholars who possess, individually and collectively, a perspective informed by the teachings of Jesus Christ. To fulfill her mission, Baylor must remain true to both components.

If we accept the idea that the transmission of knowledge developed through "scholarship with a Christian perspective" describes Baylor's mission, then I again affirm that that mission has not changed during my years here. No, I do not think the mission has changed, but the interpretation, the emphasis, and the proclamation have continually changed, in my opinion, for the better. In the following, I describe and comment on these changes (primarily scholarship) as perceived by this scientist. For convenience I sequence my historical remarks in three periods corresponding to the tenure of Baylor's presidents—the McCall years, the Reynolds years, and the Sloan years, although I think the continuity and the trend-lines are more important than any single and obvious difference in the manner by which each of the presidents approached the mission. To refer to a "scholarship discouraged, encouraged, expected" sequence as some have, while convenient and reasonably accurate, is overly simplistic.

The McCall Years: Anticipation and Disillusionment

The early 1960s were golden years for the sciences. Sputnik I was in orbit in 1957 and our government was making an all-out effort to catch up with the Soviets. The impact of Watson and Crick's 1953 description of the structure of DNA, the stuff of life, was driving the biological sciences in new directions. Rachel Carson's 1962 *Silent Spring* opened the new field of environmental science while giving to the public a fresh meaning of the old science of ecology. Science buildings were mushrooming up and faculty positions were plentiful. In such a setting, the problem facing newly minted science Ph.D.s was not the availability of jobs, but the choice of which one to take. My choice of Baylor from among a pool of state universities and liberal arts colleges was not based on any single factor—is it ever? A small college was eliminated by the teaching load and lack of research opportunity. Three universities were eliminated because of geographic location (who would want to live in the East?), and the fourth, a western university, was slow in sending a contract. So Baylor was left. My application was not based on knowledge of the academic program, but on its Baptist affiliation. Besides, everyone (read "fellow graduate students") knew about Baylor because of its football and more to the point, because of the famous College of Medicine (harken back to my comment on naiveté).

So, what was happening in the sciences at Baylor in 1966? In interview sessions with Dean George Smith and biology chair, Cornelia Smith, I learned of exciting new directions. Chemistry and physics departments had recently occupied their new building, and under construction was the new building which would house the biology department. Given the recent public awareness of water quality problems, the biology faculty had decided that the next specialty position must be in limnology. Further, the dean assured me the university was moving in the direction of graduate education and research in the sciences as evidenced by the doctoral programs in chemistry and physics and stated that the next doctoral program would be in biology. If I were to join the Baylor faculty, I would be on the "ground floor" in building the new teaching and research program in limnology and particularly the program of doctoral studies—a prospect I considered quite attractive, to say the least. Apart from the apparent opportunities in science, during the interview discussion we found a compatibility of thought relative to Christian higher education and scholarship. I expressed my opinion that Baylor, as a Christian university, had no option but to strive for excellence of scholarship. As a community of scholars, Baylor should seek to make quality scholarship the cornerstone of the school. In a Christian community of scholars an obligation to excellence is the *sine qua non*; attaching the name of Christ obligates individuals or a university to strive for excellence—to be the best they can with their God-given talents.

However, over the next few years, I slowly became aware of the gap between the administration's perception of what a university should be and mine. The absence of field and laboratory equipment was a constraint on the implementation of a research program, but thanks to the generosity of colleagues who shared their meager materials (perhaps a particular trait of faculty at a Christian university) and the presence of some exceptional graduate students, the program inched forward. And within a few years this problem was overcome with federal research grant funding. Still, the underlying drag on scholarship was more fundamental—this university existed for the teaching of undergraduate students. Anything that detracted from teaching and faculty-student interaction was to be avoided. To illustrate, I quote from a 1971 memorandum from President McCall to the faculty:

> [I]t is the policy of Baylor University that the primary function of the faculty member is to be an effective teacher. Effective teaching involves more than meeting classes. It includes consulting with and advising the students outside the classroom. I am receiving an increasing number of complaints that too many of our faculty are in effect part time teachers. . . and are never available in their offices.

Also, department chairs were not to approve any activity detracting from teaching. President McCall grouped scholarship with consulting or business activities:

> A similar procedure (Chairman approval) should be used by any faculty member now engaged in or planning to undertake any outside employment such as consultation, research or business or professional enterprises which consume substantial time and hinder the faculty member from being a full time teacher at Baylor.

In 1969 when I was granted tenure, the tenure committee's procedures document identified publication as one consideration, but it was evident that President McCall did not. In his letter granting tenure he closed with the comment, "I want to thank you for your support and assure you that the University will continue its way toward better education for its students and a better witness for the faith it represents." There was no mention of scholarship leading to the awarding of tenure or of its being expected in the future.

It was evident that under President McCall's administration scholarship was discouraged. Of course, a consequence of such a policy was to "lock in" a faculty without the capacity to compete for positions at other institutions where scholarship was expected. For many this was perfectly acceptable. For a few, it was a constant strain. On the one hand, there was classroom satisfaction with the brighter-than-average students, many of whom appreciated not only the professor's academics but also his or her presentation and discussion of the material as one Christian to another. On the other hand, there was the dismay of watching the publication record of one's cohort at other universities soar while one's own did not. This falling behind could lead to considerable self-doubt. Could it be, as Julius Caesar questioned, "The fault, dear Brutus, is not in our stars, but in ourselves, that we are the underlings"? Certainly, the more comfortable course for a faculty person at Baylor at that time was to excel in the classroom. Nevertheless, some have in their being that character attribute that Richard Feynman described in one of his most popular, and previously referenced, essays, "*The Pleasure in Finding Things Out*"—the possession of an overarching curiosity about the wonder and workings of creation, which perhaps was stifled by the "teaching only" policy.

I must not imply that Baylor University was devoid of scholarship during this period. In some of the departments, particularly those with doctoral programs, and with chair discretion, there was a certain level of research expectation and publication criteria (for promotion, not tenure) and a corresponding teaching load reduction. National recognition of these scholars ensued. In other departments, a personal drive for scholarship enabled individual faculty members to be the exceptions and earn national and international recognition.

Although not supportive of research, President McCall was highly supportive of his faculty. In the best Baptist tradition, he consistently defended our freedom of thought and speech. As a biologist teaching evolution, I know of many instances in which he fended off blows from without the university. In many cases, as I learned later, we were unaware of the attacks. Also, one must suspect that President McCall had a view of increasing scholarship for Baylor as evidenced by his recruiting the known research scientist, Herbert Reynolds, as the Vice President for Administrative Affairs and Research (and soon *de facto* President). President McCall apparently approved of the several subsequent innovations to encourage scholarship described below.

The Reynolds Years: Improvement and Convergence

My perception of President Reynolds relative to research was positively established prior to his arrival as vice president. Our first contact was made when he offered his services to the faculty as a grant proposal advisor. Early on, one of my first graduate students and I met with him in his home in Fort Worth where he advised us on the preparation of an ultimately successful federal grant proposal. It was evident that, as a research scientist himself, he was personally interested in the encouragement of faculty scholarship. This encouragement placed emphasis on the quality, not quantity, of scholarship. President Reynolds held to the belief that scholarship must be volitional—any person pursuing research because of pressure from above would likely not produce a quality product.

Although he did not, as I would have wished, make clear that scholarship is expected of any university professor, President Reynolds opened opportunities in support of research not previously available. His program as vice president and later as president was to move incrementally to increase faculty scholarship and graduate study. In the mid-1970s the program of summer sabbaticals was instituted and regularly permitted me time to undertake ecological research activities which did not require annual data. These were studies frequently funded by the University Research Committee— another benefit of his tenure. The semester-plus-summer sabbatical program was yet a further effort to encourage scholarship. Colleagues in the humanities tell me that this extended sabbatical period was particularly significant for them and "established a new climate." In the early 1980s, President Reynolds instituted the "length of service" sabbatical available to those faculty members with twenty or more years of service. Perhaps the most beneficial program to encourage research during that time was the released-time fellowships of which I received several. This program permitted a one-course teaching load reduction which, for an ecologist, was perhaps more valuable than the brief but intense period of the summer sabbaticals. Although encouraging scholarship, President Reynolds did not coerce scholarship. While desiring more doctoral programs and so informing deans and chairs, he left the decision to move into doctoral programs entirely up to each department's chair and faculty members.

Although Baylor remained a predominately undergraduate teaching institution during his tenure, President Reynolds, with his incremental approach, clearly laid the foundation that enabled the current Schmeltekopf-Sloan move to scholarship. Sometime in the early 1990s and concurrent with the arrival of Don Schmeltekopf, a perceptible transition began. It was evident to new faculty that more than good teaching would be expected of them for tenure and promotion. Through the 1980s and 1990s there was a consistent annual increase in the number of research grant proposals submitted by the faculty; however, starting in 1993 the dollar value of grant monies annually coming to Baylor increased significantly.

During this period of the 1990s there was a gradual attitude change among the faculty regarding scholarship expectations. In the 1980s I served on a departmental committee, chaired by Visiting Distinguished Professor, Joseph Hawkins, with the charge of establishing scholarship guidelines for tenure and promotion. The report of the Hawkins committee recommended criteria similar to those of research universities. The report was soundly rejected by the biology faculty. By contrast, in the spring of 1999 I was given the task of chairing another such committee. The report of this committee, which included criteria parallel to those of research universities, now serves as the guide for promotion. In the intervening years the attitude toward and expectations of scholarship had indeed changed both within the department and across the university. Within the biology department the faculty employed in the late 1980s and early 1990s were each individually interested in research—a critical mass of scholars was present and reasonable expectations of scholarship were to be accepted, not avoided.

The Sloan Years: Tier One, A Worthy Goal?

This "drift" toward scholarship at the departmental level which had characterized the later years of the Reynolds presidency was codified in 1997 when President Sloan's administration mandated that "research and scholarly/creative activity would be expected of all tenured and tenure-track faculty." Obviously, such a change in expectations would not occur without stress at the personal level. For a faculty that had based careers primarily upon teaching evaluations, this was a threat to security and self-esteem. Many were hurt and friendships regrettably were strained or broken as the scholarship criteria were employed. Nonetheless, it is difficult to see how the university could move toward what was later to be labeled as "The Vision," without such a move. The "grandfathering" of non-research faculty provided by the "A" designation,[3] although slow in coming, was an essential Christian means of addressing the human needs of the "teaching" faculty.

For those of us who opted-out of the "A" designation, this era is both a period of excitement and of concern. I am excited to see the convergence of the university's vision with the expectations I brought with me in 1966—Christians striving together for the best possible scholarship. On the other hand, after so many years of only moderate scholarly output—as judged by research universities, I must question if I am capable of "gearing-up" to meet the challenge of greater expectations, expectations of administrators, peers, and most importantly, of self.

Tier I! Is it possible? These are truly exciting times—anticipatory, stressful, challenging, but terribly exciting. And for me, long in coming. Within my discipline, limnology, things are happening with amazing speed. Twenty-some years ago, Vice President Reynolds discussed the possibility for Baylor to establish a reservoir research center, a center similar to those for natural lake studies at the Universities of Michigan or Wisconsin or Minnesota. Today that is becoming a reality both programmatically and physically in the new science building. No longer the sole aquatic scientist, I am now part of a dynamic group encompassing not only biologists, but also scholars from several other disciplines. The ecology portion of the biology department's Doctoral Program Needs Assessment proposes many opportunities for scholarship and particularly opportunities for scholarship in tropical ecology and limnology presently in Mexico and soon elsewhere in Latin America. All things *do* come to those who wait.

My excitement for the future of scholarship and the associated recognition for Baylor is not universally shared. Pessimism abounds! A major topic of discussion among faculty is the availability of a pool of scholars possessing both the requisite scholarship capacity and demonstrated Christian commitment to staff a university of this size, even if they all could be recruited. Many in the sciences doubt it (but we scientists are taught to be skeptical). We are concerned that our senior central administration has limited natural science experience and thus does not recognize how small the pool of these doubly qualified faculty may be. C. S. Lewis, who for me best embodies the enquiring Christian scholar, many years ago recognized this limitation: "Mathematicians, astronomers and physicists are often religious, even mystical; biologists *much less* often [emphasis mine]; economists and psychologists very seldom indeed. It is as their subject matter comes nearer to man himself that their anti-religious bias hardens."[4] I and many others are concerned that the overly rigorous application of a degree-of-religious-activity test will offend and turn away some competent and committed Christian scholars. While I concur with all seven criteria for faculty recruitment and hiring identified in the February 6, 2002, document from the Office of the Provost, I am concerned that the order in which they are listed suggests a prioritization, either to interviewers or interviewees. Recognition for academic excellence by national and international peers depends upon these candidates being "highly credentialed academics of demonstrated disciplinary expertise," the criterion listed fourth. While a "life of faith" (criterion #1) is highly desirable, it will have little impact on our witness if we are perceived as second-rate academics.

To paraphrase David Solomon, we can not become a "great Christian university" until we first become a "great university." And, just how is this "life of faith" to be expressed? To paraphrase the apostle Paul in writing to the churches at Corinth[5] and Ephesus,[6] there are many kinds of ministries and not all are called to overtly visible activity and service. Each individual must respond to his or her personal spiritual calling, not human pressure to conform. I believe, as did President Reynolds, that Christian participation in religious activity must, as with scholarship, be volitional. Indeed the pendulum swings. Some of us can recall faculty employed in the past who professed no relationship to Christianity or even to a Deity. However, one must ask if the pendulum has traversed beyond a reasonable position in the other direction. Having expressed this concern, I reiterate that building a world-class community of scholars who are Christian is truly a worthy goal, and, to turn once again to C. S. Lewis, "it is equally certain that a man whose mind was formed in a period of cynicism and disillusion, cannot teach hope or fortitude. A society which is predominantly Christian will propagate Christianity through its schools: one which is not, will not."[7] The "predominately Christian" phrase is consistent with the "Alternative Vision" proposed by Professor Baird.

Many of us are aware that a narrow balance exists between the Christian of Lewis' ilk and the border-line fundamentalists and creedalists, i.e., those who think they *know*. A scientist is never certain—that's the nature of science. All our knowledge is approximate, with different degrees of certainty. The agnostic Richard Feynman states it well for Christian and agnostic alike: "We absolutely must leave room for doubt or there is not progress and there is no learning. There is no learning without having to pose a question. And a question requires doubt."[8]

Attainment of such a distinguished Tier I ranking without a focus or agendum that maximizes our thin forces is unlikely. Consequently, I close this discussion with some thoughts on an agendum, primarily for the sciences, but with interactions among several other realms of scholarly endeavor. Rita Colwell, Director of the National Science Foundation, recently provided some thoughts which could serve in our attempt to focus on the future:

And so we must ask how science can elucidate these times in which we are living. We know that science brings fresh knowledge of ourselves and our planet, and, thus, what is newly possible. That, however, is not enough. Science and technology are neutral. They are neither inherently good nor bad. What we choose to do with the potential offered us by scientific knowledge is another matter. Modern biotechnology allows us to feed the world with improved nutrition but also allows terrorists to make more lethal bioweapons with greater ease.

The world has always been a delicate balance of many complex forces, not the least of which is humanity—in all of its diversity of cultures, goals, and behaviors. Today, sophisticated knowledge, powerful tools, and high-speed transportation and communication amplify that complexity. Our enterprise of scientists and engineers must be responsive to the changing context of our societies.[9]

As Baylor is now in the ten-year program of Baylor 2012, so also is the National Science Foundation in a ten-year program in Environmental Research and Education, and it has just released a ten-year outlook for the program. This document clearly shows a major change in research emphasis. The new focus is on "complex interactions," requiring a shift away from funding traditional academic disciplines to funding comprehensive interdisciplinary and multiple-disciplinary studies. I propose that Baylor develop a cohesive agendum, *Science in the Service of Humankind*, and suggest that this NSF document can provide guidance for a significant portion of Baylor's scholars. To illustrate the breadth with which NSF defines its programs we can consider the three programmatic foci:

1) Coupled human and natural systems—a focus on human health and the environment, on land, resources, and the built environment, and on environmental services and their evaluation.

2) Coupled biological and physical systems—a focus on biogeochemical cycles, on climate variability and change, and on biodiversity and ecosystem dynamics.

3) People and technology—a focus on materials and process development, on decision making and uncertainty and on institutions and environmental systems.

Any Baylor participation in successful and meaningful research in such a program clearly will encompass not only the natural sciences, but also many other departments and schools across campus.

Most scientists traditionally have not been outward looking. We are comfortable in our special narrow niches. Neither science in general nor a more focused humankind-oriented science at Baylor can so continue. To illustrate, I refer to a recent NSF-funded program on biosurfactants and toxic metal contaminants. This research involves three scientists from two universities—a microbiologist, a surface chemist, and an expert on NMR spectroscopy—to understand how biologically produced "detergents" influence the behavior of toxic metals. This suggests a model for significant science at Baylor. Not only does this research cross traditional disciplinary lines, but it also combines skills present at different universities. Involvement with colleagues at other universities is essential for much of our research, to compensate for the limited scope of science within Baylor. Such collaboration provides a means for Christian scholars here to interact with others, to demonstrate their competency, and to evidence the capacity of Christian scholars to significantly influence the world of science. If we are to be effective in our Christian witness, we first must be recognized as competent scholars, and only when that is established to be recognized as Christian women and men. To be effective, our witness should not be "in your face" Christianity. Again to quote C. S. Lewis, "Men are mirrors, or 'carriers' of Christ to other men. Sometimes unconscious carriers."[10] Certainly our Christian outreach must not be limited, as it so often is, to scientists talking to other scientists. Rita Colwell emphasized the need for scholarly scientific outreach when she said,

> We also know that in addition to generating new knowledge, it is vital that laypeople around the world and leaders from every nation have a better working knowledge of the science and technology that define our very existence on the planet. A citizenry literate about science and technology serves several goals. It gives the nation a workforce educated and trained to flourish in the increasingly demanding and competitive global marketplace. It promotes good judgment as voters on both issues and candidates. It serves as strong defense against delusions of safety as well as threats. I cannot stress enough the primary importance of a scientifically literate citizenry. I cannot stress enough the responsibility of the international science community to embrace that goal and strive to attain it.[11]

Clearly, Baylor University, with its long tradition of teaching a student body uniquely in tune with providing service to humankind, both physically and spiritually, can continue to make significant contributions to the creation of a scientifically literate society. Society in this information age is knowledge-driven, and we have come to hold great expectations for the knowledge held by science and technology.

I began this paper with observations regarding the world of science in the 1960s—Sputnik, DNA, Silent Spring. Science at Baylor was not prepared to be and thus did not become a significant global player in that exciting era. The era of tomorrow is equally dramatic and opportune for the sciences and for society. Human cloning, therapeutic and creative, with its benefits and terrors, will happen. Global environmental change will accelerate, with vast proportions of the world's population being without water and consequently without food. Investigation into the origin of life based on deep ocean capabilities will provide support of models for the origin of life elsewhere in the universe. One can go on, but the real question is: Will Baylor be positioned to be a global player in this forthcoming era? It will be challenging, but our Christian faith and Baptist beliefs demand we make the attempt.

But we also must have the wisdom to recognize that scientific knowledge alone is not going to produce a better world. Those values held by Christians in general and Baptists in particular— independence of thought embodied in the "priesthood of the believer" and evidenced in our respect for individuals—are equally essential to human progress. The scientific challenges and opportunities listed for the forthcoming era go far beyond the bounds of science. There are major social issues and major value issues that demand the scholarship of colleagues across the campus and particularly in the humanities. Please join us as scholars laboring together for the increased understanding and betterment of humankind.

Notes

---

[1] Francis Bacon, *The Advancement of Learning, Book I* (J. Spedding edition, 1854) Section VI, 14.

[2] Richard Feynman, *The Pleasure of Finding Things Out: The Role of Scientific Culture in Modern Society* (Cambridge: Persius, 1999) 102.

[3] In a policy statement issued in the spring semester 2002, all tenured and

tenure-track faculty members at Baylor hired prior to August 1991 were classified as "A" faculty, whose primary responsibility was teaching. However, any faculty member in this category could choose "B" faculty status, which provided for equal responsibilities in both teaching and research. All tenured and tenure-track faculty hired since August 1991 were classified as "B" faculty.

[4] C.S. Lewis, *God in the Dock: Religion Without Dogma* (New York: Inspirational Press, 1996) 391.

[5] I Corinthians, Chapter 12.

[6] Ephesians 4:16.

[7] C.S. Lewis, *God in the Dock: On the Transmission of Christianity* (New York: Inspirational Press, 1996) 378.

[8] Feynman 112.

[9] Rita Colwell, "Science in a Twenty-First Century World," 54th Annual Meeting of the Board of Governors, Weizmann Institute of Science, Rehovot, Israel.

[10] C.S. Lewis, *Mere Christianity, Beyond Personality* (New York: MacMillan, 1943) 163.

[11] See Colwell.

Chapter 13

Supporting the Mission: The Obligations of Faculty and Administration Alike

Ralph C. Wood

I am immensely pleased to help honor Don Schmeltekopf by participating in this colloquy that salutes his twelve-year tenure as the Provost of Baylor University. It was his visionary leadership that created the University and Distinguished Professors program, and it was my privilege to be a member of the initial class of scholars who, in 1998, joined the Baylor faculty as a result of this effort. It became immediately clear to me—when for the first time I sat across the table from the man who would soon become my new provost—that he had a clear and compelling sense of Baylor's academic and religious mission, and that it would be an enormous privilege to serve a university having such a singular and noble purpose. Five years later, I am pleased to say that I count it a high distinction not only to have reported to Donald Schmeltekopf as my immediate academic boss, but also to have counted him as a friend and companion in the things that matter most—namely, our service to Christ and his church through Baylor University.

Unlike many unordained Baptist preachers, I have only two points for my little screed. The first concerns the obligation of all Baylor faculty members to serve the university's religious and academic mission. My aim here will be to demonstrate why the requirement of active membership in a local congregation or synagogue is a freeing and not a constricting obligation. My second and appropriately dialectical thesis will deal with the administration's own no less demanding obligation to make Baylor a church-serving university. There I will offer concrete suggestions for making Baylor a more outward and visibly Christian institution.

I

Two years ago Marc Ellis, who serves as University Professor of American and Jewish Studies, arranged for several Baylor faculty to engage in a two-day dialogue with members of the Harvard Divinity School faculty. Our conversations began with a dinner at the baronial residence of Dean Bryan Hehir, a Roman Catholic. After the usual introductions and pleasantries, and after a delicious meal with appropriate libations, Don Schmeltekopf made an excellent presentation on the changes that have occurred at Baylor during the last decade. He explained that, despite the prediction that Baylor would turn secular once it became autonomous, we have sought to become at once ever more vigorously Christian and ever more vigorously academic in our intentions. He stressed the importance of administrative leadership in integrating faith and learning, especially in hiring new faculty and creating new academic initiatives. He also mentioned the enormous energy that he and President Robert Sloan have expended by interviewing every single candidate for tenure-track appointments. Then he ended his talk by presenting everyone a copy of the Baylor Mission Statement and by reading selected portions of it.

There was a long and uncomfortable silence when our provost had finished. I feared that he had embarrassed our Harvardian hosts— assuming that, from their secular standpoint, such a vision of university life must have seemed appallingly blinkered and benighted. Finally, the Reverend Dr. Peter Gomes broke the awkward stillness. Gomes serves as Minister to the University, teaches the most popular course on the campus, and fills Harvard Chapel every Sunday morning with a large congregation of worshippers who come to hear his eloquent, passionate, ethically-charged sermons. Gomes is the very embodiment of all that it means to be "Harvard"—a man of the left in almost every predictable way. He declared, to our great astonishment, that what he had just heard stirred him to three responses: admiration, envy, and caution. It prompted *admiration*, he explained, because there is no other Protestant seat of higher learning that seeks to maintain both academic rigor and Christian identity; *envy*, because Harvard would never again be able to accomplish such things; and *caution*, because—Gomes candidly warned—if we ever lose our religious mission, we will never get it back.

It is precisely this admirable and envied and irretrievable mission that all Baylor faculty are called to support—when we are hired, when we are tenured, when we are promoted, and as we continue to serve this university as long as we remain here. Far from being a crimp on our scholarly liberty, I believe that our unified religious and academic mission is what enlarges and ensures our academic freedom. Precisely as a church-related university do we have the chance to become at once academically excellent and academically free.

This claim may sound surpassingly strange, accustomed as we are to hearing that our church-connection is a threat to scholarly rigor and freedom. Let me say ever so clearly that there once *was* a serious and legitimate cause for this alarm. Those who served at Baylor during the 1980s can recall the dark days when professors in the Department of Religion were openly attacked by fundamentalists. My colleagues were accused of atheism and unbelief because they did not hold to the historical and scientific inerrancy of Scripture. They were subjected to witch-hunts by "know-nothings." This was not a threat lightly to be dismissed. Thanks, however, to the shrewdness and the courage displayed in 1990 by former President Herbert Reynolds and by his supporters on the Board of Regents, Baylor has secured its freedom from any fundamentalist take-over of our university.

Yet the freedom that we have secured here at Baylor must not be misunderstood or misused. That we are free from denominational control does not mean that we are free to become yet another *formerly* Christian school. It would be dreadful squandering of our hard-won freedom if we followed the crimson path taken by colleges and universities such as Harvard. For while they may still accomplish enormously important things—gaining, as it were, the whole world— they have lost, as Peter Gomes confessed, their religious soul. Unlike Harvard and other ex-Christian schools, Baylor is uniquely free to *serve* the church precisely because we have no cause to *fear* the church. The church does not threaten to impose on us narrowly denominational interests, confining regional biases, or prohibitive strictures against certain kinds of study—inquiry, for example, into such controversial matters as biological evolution, sexual ethics, historical causation, and the like.

If Baylor need not fear the church's constrictions, what are the freedoms it opens to us? What church is it that Baylor exists to serve, and how can service to the church not automatically constitute a threat to academic freedom? The church that Baylor exists to serve is not the Baptist General Convention of Texas, much less the Southern Baptist Convention. It is the church catholic—as the word is spelled in the lower case: the Body of Christ as it has been spread across both space and time; the *ecclesia militans* that still struggles to realize the Kingdom of God on earth; and the *ecclesia triumphans* that is yet to come at the end of space and time. Here alone, in the universal church, do we find the two things requisite: Truth large enough to ground and inspire and direct our entire academic life, and Community large enough to include everyone except those who refuse to enter it.

This community called the "church catholic" is also the community called the "church specific." It exists only in concrete instances, in tangible places, and at particular times. St. Augustine learned this lesson ever so clearly in the year 387. He had been converted to a neo-Platonic kind of Christianity. But as he struggled with the question of whether he should be baptized as a publicly avowed believer or whether he should remain a private and largely philosophical adherent of the Faith, he found himself recalling the story of two friends, Victorinus and Simplicianus. Victorinus had mastered Holy Scripture and studied all the Christian books, Augustine reports, and yet his friend Simplicianus declared that he would not count Victorinus a Christian until he saw him baptized into Christ's church. "Then do walls make Christians?" Victorinus impatiently asked.

When my students encounter this story in Augustine's *Confessions,* they answer Simplicianus's question with eager certainty: "No! Walls do *not* make Christians! We are Christians," they reply, "because we have Jesus in our hearts." So would I myself once have answered, if I had not been made to put away childish things. Surely the future bishop of Hippo and the greatest of all Christian theologians was right to give his surprising reply. "Yes!" Augustine answers in effect. "The bride of Christ *is* a terribly tawdry and compromised community. Yet Christians are made within her walls and nowhere else. Whoever will not have the church as mother cannot have God as father." This is the hard but splendid truth: there is no such thing as a solitary and private Christian. To be Christian is to be publicly identified with, to be radically dependent upon, to be utterly obligated to the Body of Christ—even when she is our Lord's shameful, prostituted Bride.

This explains why Baylor administrators ask prospective faculty not one but two religious questions. The president and provost inquire first of all about the seriousness and vitality of the professor's faith—though without having any litmus test other than the central claims of "mere" or bedrock Christianity, as C. S. Lewis called it. Yet our administrators ask a second and equally important question: they want to know about the professor's concrete involvement with and commitment to a local church or synagogue. This is no petty concern—as if church commitment were akin to civic club activity. I once recall a dean at another university declaring that he wasn't a church member because he belonged to far too many clubs already. "Thank God," I was tempted to reply, "that you've steered clear of the church."

Baylor insists on vital church membership as one of the chief means for maintaining honesty and integrity in our scholarship. So long as we have only our professional guild as our point of reference—important though it surely is—we have too small a criterion and too small an audience for our work. We have, alas, nothing larger than ourselves and our colleagues to hold us accountable. In the church, by contrast, we have been given the only trans-cultural, trans-national, trans-ethnic community. Any lesser public than this—the universal Body of Christ at work in the local church—would allow us to ask questions that are too narrow, seek answers that are too easy and, worst of all, reach conclusions that are too clandestinely idolatrous.

Against the charge that the requirement of church membership entails a sort of spiritual prying, I would answer that it is precisely what *prevents* the Baylor administration from trying to open a window into the souls of its faculty. If church involvement were *not* required, then the administration might, alas, undertake such deadly investigation. The church itself avoids all such spiritual temperature-taking. It does so by insisting that to be Christian is to be publicly identified with the Body of Christ in its two fundamental activities, neither of them private nor subjective. John Calvin called these two activities the two essential marks of the church. The church is the place, said Calvin, where the Word is truly preached and the sacraments are rightly administered. So long as we are receiving the ministry of Word and Table, it follows, our Christian life is intact.

Only as the Word of God is proclaimed to us in both its prophetic critique and its redeeming power can Christian life be sustained—including the life of private devotion and prayer. "Faith comes from what is heard," says St. Paul, "and what is heard comes by the preaching of Christ" (Rom. 10:17). Only in hearing and heeding this unique and transcendent Word are we liberated from servitude to all the enslaving establishments—whether political or religious, academic or economic. Only as we are rooted in the fundamental theological doctrines and moral practices of the church are we able to yield ourselves as living sacrifices to the Lord of life. None of these things can we give to ourselves, nor can we receive them from the academy: they are nurtured and sustained by the proclaimed Word.

So it is with the Baptism and the Supper, the two events which even we who are Baptists should be willing to call by their proper name—*sacraments.* Who among us cannot accept Luther's straightforward definition of the word? "A sacrament is a sacred sign of something spiritual, holy, heavenly, and eternal. . . . an outward and spiritual sign of the greatest, holiest, worthiest, and noblest thing[s]."[1] Baptism constitutes a fundamental transfer of our allegiance from all the kingdoms of this world to the Kingdom of God. It is in our baptism, as Luther said, that we are publicly declared the property of God. Whether in our own baptismal act or in the renewal of our baptismal vows as we witness the initiation of others into the Christian life, we affirm that we no longer belong to ourselves or to anyone or to anything else but the triune God. Even our scholarship—especially our scholarship—is owned by God and meant to serve him and his Kingdom.

So it is also with the Lord's Supper. There we perpetually acknowledge this true ownership of our lives and thus our infinite indebtedness to the good God. In receiving the broken body and the shed blood of Christ, we receive Life itself, Life in the upper case. Not to have Life but death at work in us is for our teaching and our scholarship to be either crippled or moribund or just plain dead—however lively it may seem. Sundays, therefore, should be the most important day of our week, the Day of all days, a Day like none other. For it is in worship of the holy God that we receive our literal *orientation* for the rest of the week—our vision of true East: the region of the Resurrection. To be fed by the ministry of Word and Table is to have no easy and comfortable life. On the contrary, it is to belong to a community whose existence is always a matter of struggle and contest, of doubt and agony. Authentic Christian faith makes even the most rigorous academic life seem undemanding.

Its radical demands make for radical freedom. Far from shackling our academic work, the faculty privilege of supporting Baylor's mission helps insure that our scholarship can never be stunted by small concerns. It is the church that repeatedly reminds us of the sheer grandeur of the Gospel. There we find membership in the one all-encompassing community that exists to embody this Good News. Yet the infinite scope of the church is not obvious. What begins in something exceedingly small—the call of Abraham and Sarah to be the parents of God's people—and what culminates in something smaller still—the son of a Jewish maid hanging on a cross—is, paradoxically, the largest thing in the world. Better said, borrowing from G. K. Chesterton: The Gospel is actually *larger* than the world, larger even than the *cosmos*, for it contains them both. The incarnate God alone, declares Paul, is "before all things, and in him all things hold together" (Col. 1:17).

To abandon such claims is to put not only our faith but also our learning in jeopardy. Let a single negative example suffice. At the university where I previously served, I attended a lecture sponsored by a certain cohort of the faculty. When the time came for questions, I offered what I thought were fair-minded queries about the central claims the lecturer had made. It quickly became evident that my questions were not only unwelcome but were considered rude and entirely out of bounds. Afterwards, one of my colleagues in the Religion Department upbraided me for challenging the basic assumptions of the lecturer and the audience. When I replied that such academic challenges were intrinsic to our school's very purpose, I received a strong rebuke. "Those folks were not having school," my colleague chided me, "they were having their secular church, and you disrupted their worship."

It is not only an intolerant secularism that afflicts formerly Christian schools. Derek Bok, the former president of Harvard, displays another kind of obtuseness. For him, the words "Christian" and "Jewish" are self-evidently small. He thinks that because Baylor employs only Jews and Christians, we face what he calls an "all but impossible task" in building a first-rate university. "You're ruling out," declares Dr. Bok, "a very large percentage of the ablest faculty."[2] Given our faculty hiring requirements, he predicts that Baylor may become a respectable but never a truly eminent university. What Dr. Bok cannot fathom is that there are scholars of the first order who—precisely *because* Baylor seeks to build its academic life on the unsurpassable largeness and universality of the Gospel—are *seeking* to join our faculty. They have come to Baylor from Penn State and Boston College, from Mercer and Cincinnati, from Ottawa and Wake Forest, from Calvin and Wheaton. In no case have these newcomers sought retreat from academic rigor and freedom; rather have they come in the conviction that such freedom and rigor may be found more fully here than at narrowly religious or intolerantly secular schools.

Precisely as Baylor retains its church-related mission, gladly requiring its faculty to serve the God who has identified himself in the Jews and Jesus Christ, can we avoid becoming a pseudo-church, an academic shrine, a scholarly Tower of Babel. There are *no* questions—whether moral or spiritual, whether economic or political, whether scientific or artistic—that are to be ruled out of court so long as Baylor remains a church-serving university. Precisely because the Christian narrative is a contested Story—because Christian tradition constitutes an on-going argument about matters so fundamental even as war and peace—it will always prompt disputation. It will also forbid us from bowing down before the assorted Baals of our time— the tin gods worshipped on both the left and the right. Luther put the matter ever so memorably and ever so clearly: Only in the Body of Christ, said Luther, do we remain "perfectly free lord[s] of all, subject to none," *and* "perfectly dutiful servant[s] of all, subject to all."[3]

II

To foster and maintain such biblical freedom and scholarly excellence, the administration has its own obligations. We faculty have the right to expect our president and provost and respective deans to make sure that Baylor serves the Kingdom of God in its largest ecumenical reach, not in any parochial sense. My way of putting this matter is to describe Baylor as "a Christian university in the Baptist tradition"—and not the other way around. It would be a dreadful day if we ever came to think of ourselves as more Baptist than Christian. Our commitment to the church universal must always remain our chief means of serving our sponsoring denomination.

Let me be specific. Our chief strengths as Baptists have lain in our stress on evangelism, our insistence on the baptism of the converted, our emphasis on first-rate biblical scholarship, and our devotion to the primacy of the local church, especially in its freedom from the control of worldly powers and authorities. Our chief weakness as Baptists, however, has been liturgical and doctrinal. We have often worshipped poorly and thought badly. Bad liturgy and weak doctrine make for bad ethics and weak scholarship. We need the help, therefore, of other Christians who are more adept and more experienced in both of these matters. We need, for example, the aid of our friends in the liturgical churches to assist us in learning—to cite but a single example—the dignity and the glory of worship according to the festive and penitential seasons of the Christian Year. After I have introduced the Christian Year to my Baylor students, they have repeatedly confessed how much it has enriched their lives as Christians.

We also need the help of non-Baptists in developing a Baptist theology that will preserve our unique strengths while drawing on the riches of the entire Christian tradition. We are called to work out such a theology, not only for the sake of the Baptist churches who both produced us and still sustain us, but also for the sake of the church ecumenical. Our fellow Christians who are pedobaptists need to learn the meaning and power of our distinctive Baptist attributes, chiefly our insistence on believers' baptism. It is this one doctrine that has the potential to rescue our sister churches—and, perhaps more importantly, our own Baptist churches!—from identifying the Kingdom with our nation and culture.

It is exceedingly unfortunate, I must add, that our Religion Department is not free to welcome non-Baptists to assist us in these and other important tasks—especially the task of teaching the non-Christian religions. The scholarly community currently suffers from a lack of qualified Baptist scholars who have been seriously trained in Islam and Buddhism and Hinduism. Thus are we crippled in our effort to prepare our students for living in a multi-religious world, and thus for making their thoughtful and faithful witness to the adherents of other religions. It is also embarrassing that the Department of Religion has had to abandon its prestigious Seminary Day. Dozens of seminaries and divinity schools annually sent their representatives to our campus, in recognition that Baylor produces more seriously qualified ministerial students than perhaps any other university in the country. But in order to keep representatives from the six fundamentalist-controlled Southern Baptist Convention seminaries from recruiting our students, Seminary Day has been cancelled. Only recruiters from our own Truett Seminary are allowed on campus. Together with the rule against non-Baptist groups meeting at Baylor, these two prohibitions leave the impression of a fortress mentality. Surely Baylor is not a university that fears any kind of religious challenge, and we must not leave the false impression that we do. The faculty of the Religion Department, for instance, is fully capable of making its own case in the theological arena, and we believe that our students can be trusted to make wise decisions in these matters.

For Baylor to become an ever-more ecumenically Christian university means that while our faculty should seek Baptists first and last in filling faculty openings, we must never choose a second-rate Baptist scholar over a first-rate Catholic or Episcopalian, Lutheran or Presbyterian, Methodist or Disciple of Christ, Eastern Orthodox or Jew. It also means that our campus should become more *visibly* Christian in its art and architecture. Our campus features not a single piece of sculpture devoted to a Christian subject. Between Burleson Hall and Bennett Auditorium, there once stood a statue of Jesus agonizing in Gethsemane, but it was desecrated so many times that it had to be removed. These acts of religious vandalism show how much we have to teach our students about Christian art. They are not well schooled in such matters by the one dominant campus work of alleged art—the hideously ugly fountain that students kindly refer to as "The Rocket Launcher," when they are not assigning it a more blasphemous name.

To visit St. Louis University, by contrast, is to be treated to a veritable feast of daring modern art-pieces devoted to both religious and secular subjects. Without uttering a word, these campus sculptures eloquently declare the Christian and imaginative seriousness of the university's enterprise. Baylor needs similar works of art placed all across the campus—not as mere decorative additions but as vital presences. These sculptures should be commissioned and funded with the same care and generosity that were at work in the creation of the Armstrong-Browning Library more than fifty years ago. I should add that its Meditation Room is the only space on our campus that strikes in me a real sense of the Holy when I enter it.

Yet something far costlier and more significant than campus art works is required if Baylor is to be a seriously Christian university. I am not referring to the admittedly expensive remodeling of the Tidwell Bible Building—the shabbiest and most ill-kempt edifice on the campus, an embarrassment to all of us who teach and study there. What we require most imperatively is a major architectural statement about the Christian character of our school. The new Truett Seminary building is an ever so welcome addition to our campus profile— though some unecumenical alumni have complained about the Catholic church that we have erected, simply because of the cross atop its steeple! The Truett bell tower also somberly reminds us that "Night Cometh." Together, these two architectural monuments help us to recall that we have been bought with an awful and wondrous price, and that (as Flannery O'Connor puts it) God's mercy hurries with terrible speed.

These salutary seminary pointers are helpful but still not nearly enough. Baylor needs a cathedral-like sanctuary standing at the physical and symbolic center of our common life. It need not be Gothic like the ones at Princeton and Duke, nor modernistic like the one at Valparaiso; but it does need to be large and impressive and expensive. It is in the worship of God that we are truly formed into the image of God—not only with the activities of our minds, but also with the habits of our hearts and hands, our eyes and tongues and voices. "O, taste and see," says the Psalmist, "that the Lord is good" (34:8). Our students and our faculty need a sanctuary that would enable such tasting and seeing. It would produce in us a profound sense of the holiness and otherness of God, I believe, transforming both our scholarly and religious life. At Duke and Princeton and Valparaiso, every student and professor, every parent and campus visitor—no matter how secular and unbelieving—must look up at the gigantic architectural finger pointing skyward to the Author and Finisher both of our education and our salvation.

We will need much more, of course, than the building itself. Todd Lake, our very effective Dean for University Ministries, should be given the liberty to make the new Baylor Chapel the coordinating center of all the various denominational ministries on our campus. It is a major scandal that none of Baylor's non-Baptist Christian organizations is allowed to meet on the campus, while pagan drinking clubs—sometimes known as fraternities and sororities—are welcomed. In addition to housing campus ministers from the other traditions, the chapel should perhaps have its own set of ministries to the community as well as to Baylor itself. Duke might well serve as our model. In addition to organizing a variety of weekly campus ministries at the Duke Chapel, Dean William Willimon presides over an impressive service of worship on Sundays. Not only is it liturgical and sacramental in character, it also features a powerful proclamation of the Word.

Many will no doubt charge that the erection of a monumental campus chapel—together with support required for the dean's expanded ministries—would mean that we will spend perhaps less money on new academic buildings and scholarships, even on faculty and administrative salaries. To this complaint, there is a singular and forceful answer: Exactly Right. The "uselessness" of such a sanctuary would be precisely its point. It would be dedicated to nothing other than the glory and grandeur of the God of our redemption.

An effort to raise money for the erection of such an architectural and liturgical monument to our mission is far more important, I believe, than our effort to locate the proposed George W. Bush Presidential Library on our campus. I fear that, whatever our good intentions to the contrary, this library may permanently identify Baylor with a particular political party rather than with the universal Kingdom of God. The presence of the George H. W. Bush Presidential Library at Texas A&M has forever secured the Republican identity of our sister university. Surely one Aggie Republican university is enough—indeed, more than enough! Since most of our students and many of our faculty are self-identified evangelicals, since I am myself a self-declared evangelical, and since evangelicalism has been undeniably linked with conservative politics, I am concerned that Baylor *not* become known as a conservative Baptist university. We need to make sure that no one confuses the wording on the Baylor seal—as if it read "Chartered by the *Republicans* of Texas"!

Let me make this matter clear. I have been a registered Democrat ever since I first became eligible to vote in 1964, although I have voted for the Bushes *père et fils*—though not without initial misgivings and later regret! Yet I would be just as abashed if there were a proposed Albert Gore Presidential Library to be built here rather than at Vanderbilt. I would object no less vehemently at the prospect of our becoming renowned as a *liberal* Baptist university. Surely our calling is to be a free and faithful Christian university, and therefore not identified with either right or left. An impressive chapel soaring up from Fountain Mall would help us make clear and certain that our identity is neither liberal nor conservative, neither Republican nor Democrat, but Christian.

I am concerned here with our proper Christian response to political power. "The United States," writes Leon Wieseltier, "is the strongest state that has ever existed. It has no rival, and it will have no rival for many decades. And its capabilities seem to be blinding people about its purposes. How," asks Wieseltier, "can such a powerful country not adopt its own power as its cause? How can such a mighty republic not be what Raymond Aron called 'the imperial republic'?"[4] For all people and all schools that bear the name Christian, the answer seems obvious: Our primary testimony to the most powerful nation in history must be prophetic and apostolic. We

Baptists know all too well that the Gospel has always suffered from the alliance of throne and altar, nation and church. Hence Baylor's need for a university chapel that makes powerful architectural witness by pointing away from ourselves to the transcendent and redeeming Lord of all nations and all states.

The final warning given by Peter Gomes to us who were his guests is worth repeating. "Harvard types once ran the affairs of this country," Gomes confessed, "but now it is being run by Baylor types." [I hope, of course, that he meant to say "Texas types"!] "Beware," Gomes concluded, "lest it do to you what it did to us." Harvard lost its distinctive mission when it sought to become a university serving the American project rather than the Kingdom of God. Its motto no longer reads *Veritas et Ecclesia*, but only *Veritas*. We Baptists are well-equipped to avoid such a fate. We have a long and distinguished history of keeping Christ's church free from all entangling alliances, and Baylor dare not lose this liberty. For the task of rightly ordering our loves in relation to the powers of this present age, we have a succinct Word given to us no less than to the chief Apostle: "My grace is sufficient for you, for my power is made perfect in weakness" (1 Cor. 12:9).

Allow me to conclude with a vision of the future. If the George W. Bush Library were to be dedicated here in the year 2012, four years following the sitting president's potential second term, it would serve, even at best, as a commanding public symbol of the "Pro Texana" character of our mission. Yet a lofty and reverence-inducing chapel should also be dedicated no later than that same year 2012, if we are to be serious about the first and primary half of our motto: "Pro Ecclesia." Without the latter, the former is lifeless. Only our Christian mission—the dedication of our teaching and learning to Christ's church and his Kingdom—can keep our scholarship untrammeled by lesser things: can keep it honest and vigorous, faithful and free.

Notes

[1] Martin Luther, "A Sermon on the Estate of Marriage," *Martin Luther's Basic Theological Writings*, ed. Timothy F. Lull (Minneapolis: Fortress, 1989) 633.

[2] Quoted in Vicki Marsh Kabat, "The Dilemma about Christian Scholarship," *Baylor Magazine*, Mar. – Apr. 2003: 21.

[3] "The Freedom of a Christian," *Martin Luther's Basic Theological Writings*

596.

[4] Leon Wieseltier, "Against Innocence," *New Republic,* 3 Mar. 2003: 27.

Chapter 14

How Tight to Draw the Circle?

Marjorie J. Cooper

In the following comments, I discuss several issues raised by Professors Lind and Wood in their papers. Each section incorporates my musings on a particular question that arises out of the implementation of Baylor's mission.

How Do We Support the Mission?

Owen Lind astutely observes that the mission of Baylor University has not changed over the years but that the interpretation of its mission has most assuredly changed. This, of course, is the nature of a good mission statement: it provides direction without being overly restrictive, thus allowing the organization to adapt to the ever-changing environment and its own evolving needs.

For this reason, the object of intense discussion within an organization is generally not about whether to support the mission statement, but rather about which of the various means of executing the mission the organization should employ. Thus, for Baylor the question is not whether we support the mission, but how we should support the mission in our hiring, faculty development, performance expectations, scholarly pursuits, student class size, admission policies, and all the other areas in which interpretation plays a critical role in making operational decisions. Without a consensus within the university organization on the interpretation of the mission statement, members at various levels will find it difficult to make consistent operational decisions and to send consistent messages to both internal and external constituencies.

In fact, on occasion that is exactly where various entities within the Baylor community have found themselves: uncertain as to where to draw lines concerning standards, objectives, resource allocation, and faith-based issues. In human terms, organizations pay a high price for too much ambiguity. As a result, in the controversies that we have experienced surrounding widely divergent interpretations of the mission, well-meaning members of Baylor's community describe themselves as experiencing alienation, burnout, productivity loss, career impairment, health problems, and other dysfunctions in the midst of a highly stress-laden, organizational dynamic and cultural transformation.

Without a common agreement about the essential strategies appropriate for supporting the mission, differences about operational issues rise to the surface and any unified allegiance to a broad vision statement begins to fragment. Furthermore, the consensus, or lack thereof, on the meaning of various components of the mission—for example, "Christian commitment"—will, in turn, either advance or hamper discussion centered on such tensions as unity versus diversity, structure versus freedom, and authority versus autonomy.

How Tight Do We Draw the Circle?

To protect academic freedom, to ensure that faculty members are free to develop their individual interests and expertise, and to continue to value intellectual inquiry requires tolerance for a diversity of opinions. At the same time, the desire for community and the need for a synergistic marshalling of resources and messages calls for unity. As we struggle with such tensions, it seems logical to ask, on what core beliefs and values must we have consensus in order to realize our mission? That is, how large a circle should we draw within which we designate the minimally necessary criteria for inclusion in the community at Baylor? For example, in our hiring, are those who reject the virgin birth of Christ outside that circle? What if a candidate prefers to allegorize the resurrection rather than to accept a literal, bodily resurrection? Do we place church traditions on a par with the Scriptures? Do we hire from denominations that are not considered mainstream? But more importantly, we must ask ourselves whether it is possible **not** to draw a circle. And will there ever be a circle that is not criticized by some as too restrictive and by others as too inclusive?

Two points are necessary to remember as we debate how the mission should be supported. First, we must recognize that all of us implicitly, if not explicitly, draw a circle around the beliefs we regard as essential to the mission. That is, we all have our assumptions about what it means to integrate "academic excellence and Christian commitment." We all have our notions about what is necessary and sufficient and what is not. Some circles are tighter than others, and the apparently pejorative term "creedal" seems to be applied to tight circles by those whose circles are looser. But it is disingenuous to pretend one is not drawing a circle just because one's personally preferred circle is much looser than someone else's.

Second, we need consensus on our core values to achieve a reasonable measure of support for our mission. Operational decisions will necessarily be driven by those core values and assumptions about those values. As the Lord said, "If a house is divided against itself, the house will not be able to stand" (Mark 3:25, *NASV*). So, although we all cherish our academic freedom, we are also challenged to balance that freedom with unity at some level or our mission cannot endure.

How Do We Reconcile Intellect and Faith?

There has been much discussion surrounding the recruiting and hiring of faculty who, as Lind says, possess "both the requisite scholarship capacity and Christian commitment to staff a university of this size." I think there are at least two issues implicit in hiring that we must address. The first concern is typified by Charles Malik in *A Christian Critique of the University*: "Can you serve two masters at the same time—thought and the resurrected Christ?"[1] Malik elaborates on the problem:

> It appears that something must be sacrificed here. We admire the accomplishments of the great scholars and philosophers, but we are not impressed by their spiritual state. . . I cannot imagine an Aristotle or a Kant or a Hegel falling on his knees, confessing his sins (does he have any?) and smiting his breast. I do not feel they can understand a great psalm when they read it, let alone the eighth chapter of St. Paul's Epistle to the Romans or the fourth chapter of St. John's First Epistle. And yet the intellectual accomplishments of some of these scholars and philosophers are outstanding, and some of them receive the Nobel Prize in their own fields.

Conversely, how meek and simple and spiritual and transparent some of the saints or saintly are, and yet how unsophisticated and wholly uninteresting and illiterate when it comes to sharing the great philosophical or scientific or world problems! We sit at their feet spiritually, but intellectually they are babes; they simply bore you; we cannot stay long with them; we crave the company of great intellects. . . .

So there is a problem here; truth and knowledge cannot be alien to Jesus Christ, the Eternal Logos; and yet the more we know scientific and philosophical truth the more we seem to be alienated from him; and the more we cling to him in love the more our intellectual grasp of scientific and philosophical truth appears to suffer, and the less we can converse with the great minds on an equal footing.[2]

Does a dichotomy really exist between the life of the mind and our commitment to Jesus Christ? Or, is it merely an illusion, another manifestation of the Lie? Is it reasonable to suggest that those who are in deep communion with the mind of Christ would reflect that depth of understanding in their intellectual and scholarly endeavors?

For example, Francis Shaeffer contends that study of the Bible is an asset to our intellectual life: "Do not minimize the fact that in reading the Bible we are living in a mentality which is the right one, opposed to the great wall of this other mentality which is forced upon us on every side—in education, in literature, in the arts, and in the mass media."[3]

Is it possible that we would actually be better scholars, more prolific in our process of discovery and knowledge dissemination and better able to educate future leaders if we were to incorporate the mentality of the infinite-personal God who is the author and maintainer of all the objects of intellectual inquiry? Professor Wood alludes to this possibility when he says, "Only in hearing and heeding this unique and transcendent Word are we liberated from servitude to all the enslaving establishments—whether they be political or religious, academic or economic."

How Can We Find the Best Faculty?

The second question is more obvious. Can we realistically expect to find the right people to help carry out Baylor's mission?

Admittedly, there is an economic issue of scarcity with which we must contend. But, on the other hand, as the Psalmist says,

> Unless the Lord builds the house,
> They labor in vain who build it;
> Unless the Lord guards the city,
> The watchman keeps awake in vain.
> It is vain for you to rise up early,
> To retire late,
> To eat the bread of painful labors;
> For He gives to His beloved *even in his* sleep." (Psalm 127: 1-2, *NASV*)

Problems of scarcity are in God's purview. Remember the loaves and fishes. It is not naïve or simplistic to trust the Lord to provide that over which we have little or no control; rather, it is an issue of faith. Do we believe He acts in time and space to support His program? If He does not—or cannot—then why should we be a faith-based institution? And, indeed, is this one of the necessary exercises to ensure that we remain a faith-based institution? (I don't say this lightly. I recently chaired a search committee that spent two years trying to hire a department head. During that time I prayed two prayers: (1) "Lord, give us the wisdom and patience to wait on your choice, the one You have prepared for this role," and (2) "Lord, please hurry up.")

Most assuredly we will miss out on some talented, inspiring, and highly productive individuals by hiring according to our stated mission. This is a tragedy of human fallenness—that many individuals who bear great intellectual gifts inherent in being made in the image of God have opted out of the household of faith.

On the other hand, is it possible that an uncompromising commitment to our Lord could pose a limitation to our potential as a scholarly community? Could we say that we have missed the best because of adherence to our mission statement? I do not think so. I suggest that the person who has rejected "the Way, the Truth, and the Life" by definition cannot be called one who exhibits the highest pursuit of truth. In fact, those who have committed their lives to Christ *ought* to be the most creative, insightful, and stimulating of scholars; the fact that many of us are not, as Malik has correctly observed, is an issue worth examining in our ongoing conversation.

How Do We Define Truth?

Professor Lind also raises some important epistemological concerns when he states, "A scientist is never certain—that's the nature of science. All our knowledge is approximate with different degrees of certainty."

The quest for a true community of scholars with a deep commitment to students, to the academic community, and, most of all, to Christ draws us once again into the tenuous act of balancing two important realities. On the one hand, we must avoid a narrow-minded dogmatism; on the other, we are enjoined by God's Word to certitude in matters for which we are accountable to God. For example, how many times does Paul say, "I would not have you to be ignorant"? How many times does he say, "that you may know"?

Most of us recognize that the positivism we inherited from the Enlightenment is an inadequate epistemology for determining spiritual truth in that it renders statements regarding the supernatural nonsense statements. Other tests of supernatural truth are more appropriate to theological subject matter.[4] But how do we affirm an appropriate scientific methodology for studying natural phenomena without mistakenly assuming it is the only means to truth? And can we teach our students how to tell the difference?

Notes

---

[1] Charles Habib Malik, *A Christian Critique of the University* (Downers Grove, Ill.: Intervarsity Press, 1982) 99.

[2] Malik 99-100.

[3] Francis A. Schaeffer, *He Is There And He Is Not Silent* (Wheaton, Ill.: Tyndale House Publishers, 1972) 78.

[4] See for example Norman L. Geisler, *Christian Apologetics* (Grand Rapids, Mich.: Baker Book House, 1976); J. P. Moreland and William Lane Craig, *Philosophical Foundations For A Christian Worldview* (Downers Grove, Ill.: Intervarsity Press, 2003).

Chapter 15

Let Us Not Presume: Making Room for the Loyal Critic

Byron P. Newberry

What does it mean to support the mission of Baylor University? And is supporting that mission of crucial importance? Such questions presuppose that we know what the mission is. Ralph Wood speaks of the faculty's obligation to serve the university's religious and academic mission. He then elaborates upon the religious mission. Owen Lind speaks of scholarship with a Christian perspective. His comments then focus on the academic mission. Religion and scholarship. Academics and Christian perspective. It seems self-evident to us that these are the two elemental components of our mission. And perhaps this is what Lind is referring to when he suggests that the Baylor mission has not changed over time—that our overarching aspiration is now, and always has been, the pursuit of academic excellence and achievement *in concert with* the deepening of our Christian spiritual understanding and faith.

But simply acknowledging the essence of the Baylor mission does not tell us how to accomplish it in any particular way. In fact, demonstrations of academic excellence and Christian commitment appear in an almost limitless variety, operate on many levels, and impact our world in ways large and small. Take academic excellence. It appears in challenging the most naive freshman to grapple with an old idea or a time-tested truth with which others have grappled for decades or centuries before. It appears in the startling discovery of a new truth or in the formulation of an insightful new idea about our world or about our humanity. It appears in the application of knowledge in ways that help real people solve their real problems. It appears in the creation of works of art, or music, or literature that evokes heartfelt contemplation of the beauty, or the tragedy, of this world.

These expressions of academic excellence, along with all the possible others, are largely incommensurable. Who can say which one is better, or which one will have the most enduring value? And while the works might endure, the act of achievement is itself ephemeral, like releasing doves into the sky one by one. No sooner is our accomplishment realized—our student enlightened, our idea expressed, our composition unveiled—than it moves away from us; it seeks its own place in the world, leaving us to start again.

So, too, spiritual commitment assumes myriad forms and demands continuous renewal. It is, dialectically, a journey as intensely personal as it is richly communal. Faith radiates both inward and outward. It seeks expression through divine gifts that are unique to each individual; it gains strength through the collective potential of the community that is the church catholic, of which Ralph Wood speaks. Our Christian faith—our need and our duty to understand and to cherish both creator and creation—gives rise to and gives meaning to our academic enterprise; and the fruits of our academic enterprise affirm and enlarge our understanding of what it is to be Christian. We join together in the church to express in unison our shared belief. At the same time we each tread our own path, finding our own distinctive ways in which to live as we are called to do. As educators whose job it is to speak and to serve, we could find no better words to guide us than these of 1 Peter 4:11: "If anyone speaks, he should do it as one speaking the very words of God. If anyone serves, he should do it with the strength God provides."

So, yes, I want to affirm and to celebrate Baylor's religious and academic mission. And I believe that supporting that mission, in all the richness and texture of its many meanings and manifestations, should hold a central position in the heart of every Baylor faculty member. But this affirmation of our mission still does not solve the problem of understanding how one *demonstrates* support for it. How can we tell if someone does not support the mission of the university, short of his or her expressly disavowing any interest in either academic excellence or religious faith? This question takes on added urgency in our present time of change. But if the mission of the university has not changed, what has changed? Owen Lind says it is the interpretation and implementation of the mission that has changed. No single institution, much less any individual person, could ever hope to accomplish all the things that are possible under the heading of academic excellence and religious faith. So we set priorities. We can't do it all, so we say, "*this* and *that* are what we will try to do best." Lind has chronicled the shift in priorities over the span of his tenure here, culminating most recently in Baylor 2012.

But priorities are things which lend themselves to disagreement. I think doing X is most important, and you think doing Y is most important. But this is not a bad thing. Rather, it is vital to having any hope of our moving in the right direction. Healthy debate and respectful dissent are the gyroscopes that keep nudging, perhaps sometimes shoving, the institution back onto its proper course. In a recent *Chronicle of Higher Education*, Charles Evered notes, "institutions are like families. Some encourage free expression, and some shut down, especially in crisis, and encourage conformity. It seems to me that those colleges that encourage only one line of thought become lazy, incestuous, and smug." Stephen Evans speaks of *contested goods*. The religious and academic mission of the university is a contested good in the truest sense. We agree that the mission is vital to our flourishing, but we can have, and should have, sustained argument as to how it is to be accomplished.

Ralph Wood gives an impassioned argument for why Baylor faculty members need to be active participants in a church. Robert Baird gives an equally impassioned argument for why this need not always be the case. We can disagree about which point of view would be the most efficacious for accomplishing the Baylor mission. While I embrace Baird's approach, others of you would prefer Wood's. But of one thing I am sure. Both of these men believe in, care about, and support the Baylor mission with their hearts and minds. Though their words conflict, each one speaks as if speaking the very words of God. In fact, I believe the most avid proponents among the faculty of Baylor 2012 are enthusiastic supporters of the mission of the university. But I also believe that the most vigorous critics among the faculty of Baylor 2012 are enthusiastic supporters of the mission of the university. Wood speaks of his desire to see a massive, symbolic religious sanctuary in the center of campus. If I understand his point correctly, that sanctuary would serve as a reminder that we at Baylor are free to ask any question and to seek any answer, precisely because the divine power symbolized by that sanctuary has nothing to fear. By challenging every assumption, by dissecting every premise, we cannot diminish it; we can only strengthen it. As Evans said during yesterday's discussion, "loyalty may require us to be a critic."

I am particularly sensitive to the fallacy that differences of opinion reflect support or non-support for the university's mission. I have had the opportunity to serve on the University Tenure Committee during the time when the campus community has been discussing and implementing Baylor 2012. I have read colleague evaluations of tenure candidates in which the authors have made vague and weakly supported statements to the effect, "I don't believe that 'so-and-so' really supports the mission of the university," with the implication being that "so-and-so" has expressed criticism of, or concern about, one or more aspects of Baylor 2012. I have to believe that voicing criticisms and concerns with respect to Baylor 2012 is not only allowable, it is required. Do we really want to follow a plan so important to our future without having subjected it to the closest scrutiny?

Baird quotes the provost of Notre Dame as saying, "we have never felt comfortable weighing someone's spirituality." Well, I don't feel comfortable weighing someone's support for the university's mission. I believe such statements as I alluded to on a tenure evaluation are grossly disingenuous. Tell me how a candidate has not demonstrated competency in teaching. Tell me how a candidate has done shallow or slip-shod research. Tell me how a candidate has shirked responsibilities for service to the department or the university. Tell me how a candidate has failed to treat students or colleagues with the love and respect requisite of someone attempting to live his or her life in accordance with Christian ideals. But don't tell me that he or she doesn't support the university's mission simply because he or she has expressed disagreement about some shift in policy of which you were in favor.

So, then, here are my answers to the initial questions. What does it mean to support the mission of Baylor University? It means having a commitment to academic excellence and spiritual understanding in the broadest sense. Is it important to support in principle the mission of the university? I believe it is. Is it our obligation to support in practice the mission of the university by performing to the best of our ability those tasks which the university has set as priorities? I believe it is. Is it important to challenge respectfully those priorities with which we disagree, provided we believe an alternate path is truly the better one? I believe it is. But when it comes to plumbing the depths of someone's soul to determine whether he or she truly supports Baylor's mission, I can only respond cautiously with the words of J. Alfred Prufrock: "How should I presume?"

Chapter 16

Baylor's Shared Baptist Vision

Roger E. Olson

Ralph Wood is concerned to make sure that Baylor becomes an even more outwardly and visibly Christian institution than it already is. Owen Lind is concerned that the university's Christianity not be too "in your face." I take him to mean that it avoid becoming overly overt and obvious so as to diminish the university's scholarly reputation and ability to draw excellent scholars to its faculty. Both concerns possess some validity. Not long ago I taught at a Christian liberal arts college that is openly and unapologetically Christian; it promotes itself as an evangelical college. However, its showcase building—the Community Life Center—notably lacks any religious symbolism, even though it functions as a chapel as well as a concert auditorium. I was told that no religious symbols would be allowed on its exterior or interior in order not to offend the community which is largely secular and pluralistic. The danger of failing to be as visibly Christian as one intends and claims is real; it must be recognized and resisted.

On the other hand, Lind's concern is valid. I taught at another Christian university some years ago where the founder and president spoke *ad infinitum, ad nauseum* about "joining prayer and medicine" in the healing process. He founded a school of medicine and built a hospital and research center for that purpose. I decided it was time to leave when I heard him speak in chapel about sending seminary students into the laboratories to lay hands on experiments and pray for them. He didn't say "experimenters," he said "experiments." Needless to say, that university had trouble recruiting even Christian professors and doctors for its science programs after that. There are limits to credibility that must be respected, even and perhaps especially by Christian institutions in a culture dominated by naturalism (to say nothing of common sense!). On a much less sensational level, I recently waited in a local physician's office waiting room and noticed that every book and magazine there was explicitly Christian. On the walls were several overtly Christian quotations and mottos. Bible passages adorned the walls of examining rooms. Even as a Christian theologian I found myself vaguely uncomfortable as I wondered how a non-Christian might feel in such surroundings. I'm certainly not opposed to letting one's Christian identity be known, but in the process we should avoid triumphalism that makes prisoners of our audience and imposes our beliefs on them without their consent.

I find myself in some agreement with Wood's concerns and also with Lind's concerns. I also have some concerns of my own about their proposals.

I agree wholeheartedly with Wood that tenure-track and tenured faculty members of a Christian institution should support its mission by being actively engaged with Christian churches (or Jewish synagogues in cases of Jewish members of the community). Christianity is not an individualistic religion or philosophy; it is communal and the church is its primary communal expression. Claiming to be Christian while abandoning the church is simply hypocritical; "Lone Ranger Christianity" is an oxymoron. The church, with all its flaws, is a source of life for Christians and for Christianity. I also agree with Wood that Christianity has cognitive implications—it is fair and right for a Christian university to expect its faculty members and administrators to be committed to basic Christian beliefs and values. (An exception applies to Jewish members of the community who should be committed to Jewish beliefs and values which largely overlap with Christian ones.) Finally, I agree that Baylor should strengthen its catholic and ecumenical ties: it should be Christian first and Baptist second.

I would like to argue, however, that Baylor should retain its sectarian identity. By "sectarian" I merely mean "free church" as opposed to "magisterial church" which is closely linked to Christendom. These are historical categories. One of Baylor's strengths is its populist religious and social ethos, rooted in a strong sense of a non-hierarchical religious community free of creedalism, spiritual coercion, and clerical control. Baptists with education, wealth, and prestige are noted either for becoming Presbyterians or

Episcopalians or for imitating them. I have nothing against either of those Christian traditions, but I value being Baptist and preserving the Baptist ethos. What is that ethos? At its heart stands a vision of the regenerated individual in community and of a religious community of compassion and accountability. I am not one of those moderate Baptists who thinks unrestricted freedom is the hallmark of Baptist faith and life, but I do believe that the Baptist witness to the world and to other Christian traditions includes a distinct vision of what it means to be an individual before God within community and what it means for a Christian community to worship and work collaboratively and compassionately without hierarchy. What is more important to me than whether a cathedral stands at the center of the campus is that Baylor preserve and strengthen its respect for individuals, its community spirit of compassion and accountability, and its fierce Baptist independence from government and freedom from even covert forms of episcopacy.

The issue here is not, as I see it, denominational affiliations of faculty members or administrators. The issue is more subtle, even as it is more important. It is the issue of culture and ethos. I hope that as Baylor pursues its vision of greatness, it finds ways to highlight and strengthen its evangelical, free church, Baptist heritage and identity without falling into a sectarianism that pretends any denomination has a monopoly on authentic Christianity. One way to do that would be to house within the cathedral at the center of campus a vital, well-endowed, high-profile Center for Baptist and Free Church Studies to which scholars of many different denominations come for sabbaticals, research, teaching, and lecturing. The Center would offer to members of the Baylor community and to the larger church universal conferences and lectureships on what it means to be Christian in the modern and postmodern world and on the uniquely Baptist and free church spin on that.

I agree with Lind that Baylor must try to avoid needlessly alienating the larger scholarly community with a kind of overtly and triumphalistically religious posture. However, I disagree if he means to say that Christian faith and Christian commitment require a kind of certainty that excludes doubt. This is apparently one of his qualms about giving Christian commitment a high profile in the university: it seems to conflict with the scientific commitment to questioning and doubting as part of the discovery process. I take it he is worried about the perception if not the reality of "blind faith" governing our intellectual life and research. As Paul Tillich argued, however, the dynamics of true faith include doubt. Frederick Buechner put it more humorously: "Doubt is the ants in the pants of faith; it keeps it moving." British bishop and missionary statesman Leslie Newbigin emphasized that absolute certainty is not a human possibility and that Christian faith and commitment are based on "proper confidence" rather than God-like epistemological certainty. If I understand matters at all correctly, all that Baylor expects of its faculty members in this regard is that they say, "I believe; help Thou my unbelief." But a Christian university must ask its faculty members to take the finite risk of believing. To believe in what? In the unity of reality in a personal Creator and in the redemption of creation by Jesus Christ, the world's Savior and Lord. That commitment does not require certainty that excludes doubts and questions; it only excludes chronic skepticism and outright denial of the Christian story. It certainly does not include any hocus-pocus about praying over cancer research experiments for supernatural discernment about which ones are likely to produce results. It does require belief in the transcendent source of life, meaning, and value; it requires belief that technology is not the master but a servant. It requires belief that no discipline is an end in itself but that every human study gains its value by glorifying God and helping human beings enjoy Him forever. And it requires a steadfast determination to see all of reality as the theater of God's glory, searching out the connections that tie faith in Him to our world and our world to faith in Him.

I suspect that Lind agrees with this, but I sense a certain understandable nervousness in his presentation that perhaps Baylor's mission (or some interpretation of that mission) calls for something more that borders on excessive intrusion of the spiritual into the natural. I too would reject any diminution of the sciences' hard evidentialism. However, every research project involves some interpretive vision of the world, that is to say, some faith. Baylor's shared interpretive vision is the classical Christian one, and there is nothing about it that hinders scientific research because it is *not* of the fundamentalist variety. What it excludes is a secular and naturalistic world view that ultimately ends in nihilism And it excludes belief that science is an end in itself rather than simply a servant of humanity created in the image of God. Therefore, Christians in the sciences must ask about the ethical implications of research and invention and not only about their pragmatic results. Baylor's mission is not against science but only against scientism. This is something we need to communicate to ourselves and to our external constituencies—including the wider scholarly and scientific worlds—with conviction and persuasive power.

Chapter 17

Conclusion

The Renewal of Christian Higher Education

David Solomon

As always it is good for me to come back to Baylor. It will be forty-three years ago in September when I moved into the second floor of Kokernot Hall North and commenced my Baylor education. I had not wanted to be here. I had wanted instead to go to MIT and become an engineer. My mother had other ideas and worked out my admission to Baylor with little cooperation from me. After my mother died, I found a correspondence in her letters with W. C. Perry, dean of students at Baylor at the time I was admitted. My mother had started adult life as a country school teacher somewhere over by Lampasas where Dean Perry had then been the principal. In the correspondence, my mother explained to Dean Perry that she did not want me going to some East Coast school since I was already pretty confused and an East Coast school might finish me off. Dean Perry wrote back that if she could get me to Baylor, Baylor could take care of the rest. In reading this letter, I was unclear what "the rest" referred to, but I guess Dean Perry and my Mom understood it. She got me here on a Texas Bus Company bus from Walnut Springs. Baylor took care of the rest, and I am deeply grateful for the graces bestowed upon me during my years here. Those graces came through the teaching and influence of many people at Baylor, Ralph Lynn and Ann Miller, Rufus Spain and Clement Goode, Bud Duncan and Bob

Reid, and countless friends. Others, no longer with us, were also memorable, especially Bill Toland, Jack Kilgore, and, above all for me, Haywood Shuford.

I

We are here to do two things—first, to celebrate the career of Don Schmeltekopf, and second, to do it by having a knock-down drag out argument. This is a curious tradition in academic life to honor a beloved colleague by arguing over his bones—not that Don has been reduced to mere bones quite yet. Let me begin by saying a few things about Don, and then I will ease into the argument.

I have said on a number of public occasions, and I am happy to say it again tonight, that Don Schmeltekopf is the most important figure in Christian higher education in the last decade of the twentieth century. I said this recently at a meeting of a group of Catholic scholars, and someone shouted from the audience, "What about the Pope?" That seemed to me to prove my point. Any Baptist who even gets compared to the Pope is a big deal. Besides, the Pope, although a great man, never held a job in American higher education—at a Baptist school and in a tumultuous decade—and survived simultaneous attacks from fundamentalists and progressives (or whatever we now call Baptists who aren't fundamentalists but aren't liberals either). Don has done all of these things, and he has also set the fire of revolution.

Baylor was not exactly on the front page of the debates over Christian higher education a decade ago—a sleepy Southern university that every ten or fifteen years would beat Texas at football, happened to produce a super fast runner who looks really weird when he runs, and makes the *New York Times* every decade or two, either by canceling a controversial dramatic production written by one of the greats of the American theater, or by censoring photo spreads of comely coeds in men's magazines, or by not doing anything that has to do with drinking or dancing. If you are a Baylor graduate, whenever you told your friends where you were from, they always paused and then said, with a little smile, "Yeah . . . I remember Baylor." Don Schmeltekopf (along with a few others) has changed all that. Now, of course, they do sometimes say, "Do you know Schmeltekopf? Is he for real?" Or more likely, "What's really going on at Baylor? Are they serious? Do you think they can pull it off?" And everybody knows what "it" means, and it has nothing to do with drinking or dancing. Baylor very generously sent a number of students to a conference we had at Notre Dame last year at which President Robert Sloan participated in a panel regarding the future of Christian higher education, together with our president, Father Edward Malloy, and an old student of mine, Charles Dougherty, who is now president of Duquesne. The Baylor students were pleasantly surprised, I think, that it was Baylor—not Notre Dame and certainly not Duquesne—that generated the most discussion and the most interest. Don Schmeltekopf has changed the perception of Baylor in the world of higher education and in our culture at large. He asked questions wherever a few were gathered together to talk shop about Christian higher education, especially at such important meetings as those sponsored in the last decade by the Lilly Foundation. Sometimes he would even answer his own questions—or correct the answers of others. And if he still wasn't satisfied, he was known on occasion to raise his already considerable voice a decibel or two and—I hate to report this back on the home campus since I am sure you have never seen anything like this—he pounded the table. On one visit to my house, Don, at the dinner table where we were gathered arguing about these matters, pounded so hard that a fine piece of crystal took flight and was saved only by the quick hands of Mike Beaty, who I believe came along to catch flying china. We now add a thicker pad at the table when Don is in town.

What did Don ask about and how did he ask these questions so that Baylor is now talked about and thought of in a quite different way? Don wanted to know what could be done to prevent the complete secularization of American higher education at the university level. When he started asking this question, secularization was complete in Europe and was almost complete in this country. No one even remembered that Northwestern and Southern California had been Methodist, or that the University of Chicago had been founded with Rockefeller money in the 1890s as a Baptist university. Some people knew, but hardly anyone cared, that Woodrow Wilson's Princeton had been Presbyterian. The massive studies of this phenomenon by scholars like James Burtchaell, George Marsden, and others had documented and begun to explain this shift. Notre Dame, among the Catholic remnant, had been responding to secularization over the past couple of decades, supported by a remarkable president, Father Theodore Hesburgh, and the deep pockets of the Notre Dame alums. (Endowment went from under $50 million when I arrived at

Notre Dame in 1968 to almost $4 billion before the stock market took back its share a couple of years ago.)

From the beginning, Don has taken Notre Dame as an example for Baylor to follow, not, of course, on matters of the sacraments or ecclesiology, I hasten to add (Don has been accused of many things but never, as far as I know, of being a crypto-Papist), but on matters of educational strategic planning, faculty issues, and curricular development. I have at other times compared Notre Dame's move in 1966 (orchestrated by Father Hesburgh) to transform itself into an autonomous private university in the Catholic tradition to Baylor's dramatic charter change of a decade ago. Just as some thought that Notre Dame's move in 1966 signaled the secularization of Notre Dame, many thought that Baylor's move in 1990 signaled the secularization of Baylor. In both cases, of course, these critics were wrong and dramatically wrong. After the 1965 Land of Lake's meeting at which clerical control of Notre Dame was removed, Father Hesburgh built one of the most dynamic universities in this country. He revitalized faculty hiring (I was part of that revolution, being only the third non-Catholic hired in the philosophy department), created a co-ed student body, raised money at a rate unprecedented in Catholic higher education, transformed the physical campus, and all in the name of building a vital Catholic university. Father Hesburgh's slogan, oft repeated, was, "If we want to be a great Catholic university, first we must be a great university." He sold that slogan to the sons and daughters of Catholic immigrants who had built the blue-collar industries of the rust belt, and they financed the Hesburgh revolution.

Notre Dame was the great success story in the world of Christian higher education when Don started asking his questions at those Lilly meetings in the 1990s. But we are not here to talk about Notre Dame, but rather to talk about Baylor and Don Schmeltekopf's dynamic role in its rise to national prominence in the last decade. Don, by the early 1990s saw a number of things clearly, I think, that many others did not see—or if they saw them, they didn't talk much about them. He saw, first, that Christian higher education at the university level was in deep trouble and, second, that Notre Dame's intentional administrative actions to preserve Christian character were essential to any long-range plan that had any hope of success. If universities were allowed to drift, that drift went in only one direction.

He also saw two other things: that Baylor was the only Protestant research university in this country that had a chance of becoming a great Christian university. Duke and Vanderbilt, along with the Ivies and other great universities formerly Christian, could not come back; outstanding Christian colleges like Calvin, Wheaton, and Valparaiso couldn't leap to university status; and other Protestant universities like our neighbors SMU and TCU lacked the will or the substance for any significant change. Finally, Don saw clearly that the key to making Baylor the great Protestant research university it could be lay in the management of faculty hiring. Following the Hesburgh mantra and following steps already taken by Herbert Reynolds (as so neatly explained in Owen Lind's paper), Don wanted Baylor to be both a great university and a Christian university. As Mikeal Parsons puts it, he wanted to raise both bars at once. Here the secularization of research universities in this country was doubly unfortunate. First, as we have seen, these universities were secular in themselves with all that meant for the direction of research and curriculum, but also these secular universities were training Ph.D.'s in a thoroughly secular atmosphere and then sending out their graduates to teach at Baylor and Notre Dame. They were not only poisoned with secularism themselves, they were also exporting the poison.

Indeed, this is surely the way secularization moved throughout American higher education earlier in the century, radiating out from the great research universities restructured at the end of the nineteenth century on the German model. This movement constituted a kind of evangelization of American higher education in the name of secularization. Don said, and repeated *ad nauseam*, that unless one could have a faculty broadly committed to the ideals of a Christian university (and with that commitment rooted in rich Christian practices), any other efforts to retain Christian character would be futile. We might call this "The Schmeltekopf Doctrine." He took that idea so seriously that he extended it to the truly outrageous idea of interviewing at the level of the central administration all candidates for faculty positions at Baylor. In these interviews he actually asked candidates about their religious practices, names of their churches, and their plans for church involvement if they came to Baylor. I will return to some reflection on the wisdom of this in a moment, but for now I want simply to call attention to how bold and incendiary an action this was. When it became clear that Don was not only doing this, but also taking steps to confirm what candidates had said, many were outraged while many others took this as a simple sign that Don actually meant what he said (which, when you think of it, is quite an extraordinary thing among university administrators).

One of Don's finest moments, I think, was at Notre Dame when he stated and defended his views on these matters at a little conference we arranged on the Friday afternoon before the Baylor/Notre Dame football game played on Reformation Day, October 31, 1998. (This conference and game are remembered by many as the only conference depicted in a novel written before the conference occurred and published on the opening day of the conference. This novel, *The Lack of the Irish*, was written by my colleague, philosopher and novelist Ralph McInerny.) At the central session of this conference, Don and our provost, Nathan Hatch, a formidable Protestant scholar in his own right, talked about their conceptions of how hiring should be managed at universities serious about their Christian character. It would be unseemly, not to say imprudent, for me to pick a winner in that gentle debate (Nathan Hatch is still my boss), but let me say that Don's presentation was marked by plain speaking, an uncompromising defense of a clearly articulated policy, and an eloquent statement of Baylor's vision of the future. Many thought after the session that the title *The Lack of the Irish* was appropriate for this exchange, even if not quite right about the football game the next day. People left that session inspired and invigorated, but a little nervous. A year or so later, one of my colleagues reminisced about the discussion and said, "That guy from Baylor was really something; you know the one who sounded sort of like a cowboy." Don, as usual, had pounded on the table a couple of times, but fairly gently and in a manner appropriate to academic wrangling.

This is not, of course, the full case that can be made for my claim that Don Schmeltekopf is the most important figure in Christian higher education in the 1990s. More needs to be said. He was, of course, not alone in these efforts. President Reynolds had in many ways gotten the ball rolling, and that other President, Robert Sloan, had some hand in this transformation, too, as well as many other people in this room tonight. But tonight is Don's night, and I am not going to worry about being fair to the rest of you.

Don had a number of virtues that made him perfectly suited to bring this issue to the attention of university administrators, faculty, and other interested parties. He was stubborn and relentless in pushing these issues. He refused to be taken in by the kind of soft-minded optimist one encounters so frequently in discussing these issues (deck of the Titanic optimism). He always kept the big picture in front of his audience—and secularization was the big picture. He was not intimidated by the pseudo-sophistication of those who condescended to him and his message as coming from the fringe—geographically and ideologically—of the contemporary university scene. Ralph Wood talks of the profound impression Don made when talking to a group of Harvard faculty a few years ago. I have been present on many occasions when he similarly impressed audiences with the directness, the sincerity, and the persuasiveness of his message. He was the right man, in the right place, at the right time.

II

I would like to turn briefly to discuss a number of points that emerged in the colloquy papers that impinge on Don Schmeltekopf's vision of a new kind of Christian higher education. First, an important point that both Robert Baird and Parsons make. They note that Baylor is trying not only to revitalize its Christian character but also to transform itself into a first-tier research university emphasizing research responsibilities for the entire faculty.

Baird is primarily worried about how this emphasis on research and scholarship might affect Baylor's traditional commitment to excellence in teaching. I share this worry. None of us is doing a very good job at this, and I wish Baylor well in dealing with these problems.

The problem that worries me more, however, is the difficulty in preserving and nurturing a Christian faculty while also hiring at the very highest levels. When there are few Christian candidates for positions to begin with, the extra pressure put on the hiring process to deliver both the best candidates—or at least those that will put you in the top rank—and the Christian candidates can be enormous. When a university decides to be really good, moving up through the rankings, a logic takes over that is not unlike the logic of recruiting for big-time athletics. Notre Dame likes to have guys named Flanagan or O'Rourke on the football team, but that is something we can seldom do. Christian character is almost always a casualty of the pursuit of athletic excellence, and some comic incidents have resulted from our attempts to integrate Catholic practices into the life of our largely non-Catholic athletic staff and teams. Our worthy, but Protestant, new football coach, Tyrone Willingham, was presented with a miraculous medal at some occasion early in his career at Notre Dame, and he has been seen with it laced into his sneakers that he wears to practice. This is no doubt the way new religious practices are born. I look forward next year to religious medals on the chin straps of the player's helmets and holy water in the Gatorade bucket.

But Christian character is also frequently a casualty of the pursuit of academic excellence. The philosophy department at Notre Dame is ranked thirteenth in the country. At our last outside evaluation, the evaluators were instructed by our administration to tell us what we need to do to be in the top ten.[*]

But I doubt that Notre Dame can be in the top ten and retain our commitment to be a Christian philosophy department. A couple of anecdotes demonstrate this problem. We recently had a fuss in our economics department that made the *Chronicle of Higher Education*. We have traditionally had great strength in development economics (what we call "rice-paddy" economics) that fits well with our commitment to the tradition of Catholic social teaching. This is not, however, the part of economics that gets you highly ranked among economics departments. For that you need to turn to econometrics and the more highly mathematicized branches of the discipline. Our rice-paddy guys fit well with the Catholic mission, they are the best teachers in the department, but they are not the future. They don't publish in the right journals and we want to be number one.

Another anecdote. We were hiring for a position in philosophy this year for which we had three superb candidates, all women, all from top-notch graduate programs, all with dissertations directed by leading scholars in the field. To my eye, from the standpoint of scholarly promise and excellence, any would have been a superb hire. One was a practicing Catholic, indeed, a former student of ours as an undergraduate, one a practicing and serious Episcopalian, and one a thoroughly secular candidate with no interest or, it seemed, aptitude for religion. The specialists in the area were delighted with these

---

[*] As an aside, there is no big secret to moving up in the rankings, of course, and most of us know how to do it. We simply buy the people that will put us there. It is the same way that baseball teams win pennants. When Carl Vaught was at Yale in 1965, it was the best philosophy department in this country. By 1975, it was not even in the top twenty. This is not because, as Vaught says, that he left Yale, but because the University of Pittsburgh bought the entire Yale philosophy department (or at least that part of it worth buying) and thereby earned themselves, among philosophers in the know, the nickname "the Pittsburgh Pirates." As I said, just like in baseball, Pitt got to be number one and Yale has been languishing in the wilderness ever since.

candidates and ranked them with regard to research potential as follows: secular candidate, first; Episcopalian, second; Catholic, third. With no real discussion of their overall suitability for Notre Dame, we made the offer to the secular candidate, who kept us waiting a few weeks and then turned us down. By that time the other candidates had taken positions elsewhere.

Scholarly standards trumped everything else in the hiring process in this case, and it is becoming increasingly difficult to argue against this kind of resolution of faculty hiring cases at Notre Dame. It behooves you at Baylor, I believe, to think hard about how you will hold scholarly excellence (and disciplinary prestige) together with the demands of Christian character. There is no doubt that Notre Dame's academic success—and its deep longing for even more—is the greatest threat at this moment to its Christian character. The student body at Notre Dame is 85 percent Catholic, the religious life in the dorms is rich and influential on students, and the opportunities for Christian service are greater there than at any other university in the country. The faculty, though, under the pressure to move up the rankings (rankings established by the secular academy), is becoming increasingly secular. Some think that if the campus is permeated by the religious, the nature of the faculty will be relatively unimportant. On this issue, I stand firmly with Don Schmeltekopf. The faculty determines ultimately the character of a university. They are the only ones with genuine job security, for one thing. They can frustrate, if they wish, any administrative ploys. They remain the greatest influence on students' beliefs and character.

Baylor wants to enrich its Christian character, be a great teaching university, and move up the disciplinary rankings. This isn't easy. If Notre Dame is a secular university in fifty years, they should burn into the grass on the main quad, "Standards made us do it."

III

Parsons proposes that we take seriously a model for determining who should be hired at a Christian university that he calls the "significant contribution model." Some might object, however, that the notion of "significant" is hopelessly vague and can't serve as an appropriate measure. This objection is similar to one that we at Notre Dame encountered when we proposed that the right measure of how Christian a faculty should be is that it involve a "preponderance." "Significant" contribution is as ambiguous as is "preponderance."

Our logicians screamed about this, asking for precision (of course, these are the same guys who can't get their peanut butter on the cracker). Why should we want precision? We are instead going to have to have an argument. We must face the fact that none of us knows what a Christian university for the next millennium will look like—not even Don Schmeltekopf—and to his credit he has never pretended to know. What he has wanted is to give us a fighting chance, institutionally, to figure out what a Christian university can be in the post-Christian West.

Stephen Evans rightly argues that we should not try to build Newman's university; we certainly cannot build, as my colleague and friend Ralph McInerny would like, Aquinas's university; I hope nobody is foolish enough to try to build John Calvin's university, although my colleague Al Plantinga looks wistfully out the window when the prospect is mentioned. Tom Monaghan, the Domino's pizza man, is trying to build a real Catholic university (and he has a billion dollars), but it is becoming increasingly clear, I fear, that his main ideas don't go far beyond a zesty sauce, a crispy crust, and an on-time delivery. (One of my colleagues who was being interviewed for a position at Ave Maria, as this university is to be called, tried to remonstrate with Mr. Monaghan about his dress code for faculty, and she was told that it had done wonders for the on-time delivery service. I hesitate to give this idea to Don—one you forgot about.) I proposed a number of years ago that the only way we can flesh out these vague concepts like "significant" and "preponderance"—place holders for argument—is to put a lot of smart and faithful Christians in one institution, give them enough resources with which to work and enough bright and energetic students whom they can teach, and let her rip! I still don't see any other way to proceed. This is a tactical proposal—and it is exactly Don Schmeltekopf's. The "let her rip" part has also excited a lot of us, and it flies in the face of the criticism of Don's efforts that they will lead to reactionary or conservative university life. Nothing could be farther from the truth.

IV

The themes that Baird discusses are going to provide the final focus of my comments. Baird, I think, puts as clearly, directly, and as convincingly as it can be put what the objections are to many of the policies Baylor has committed itself to follow in the coming years. Second, I know of no person whose opinion on this matter I value more.   Bob Baird was already at Baylor when I came here as a seventeen-year-old freshman.   He knows Baylor as well as anyone could, and what he doesn't know, Alice can tell him.   He is also as good a man as I know, and he loves Baylor and loves it in that sense of love explicated by Aquinas where to love something is to be concerned to "care for its good."   It pains me that I disagree with his overall conclusion, but I do, and I want to say why I do.   But I also want to say why I think he is right about another issue which is perhaps more important than the narrower one about which he and I disagree.   I want to confront the Baird position with the Schmeltekopf position and argue that while Baird is right about the appropriate strategy for building a great Christian university, Schmeltekopf is right about the tactics.

What are Baird's main claims?   There are four of them:

1) He claims that the religious identity of Baylor is secure and says, "I see no evidence that its ongoing security needs a more rigorous examination of the religious commitments of prospective faculty."

2) He then introduces three enormously attractive figures, two of whom were my former teachers, Charles Hartshorne and Haywood Shuford, who he claims exemplify those who would be unhirable at Schmeltekopf's Baylor, could not be hired at Notre Dame, but who would be valuable members of the faculty.

3) He reminds me, in a kind of Notre Dame low blow, that Notre Dame has combined academic excellence with religious faithfulness without resorting to the kind of draconian investigations associated with the Schmeltekopf plan.

4) And, most persuasively, he paints a picture of a Christian academic community religiously secure but open to the full range of dissenting views on intellectual matters.

Baird raises so rich an array of issues in such a persuasive way that it would take far too long to respond to them all.   He and I have been arguing about these matters for years and I would like to make a few remarks in response, however inadequate these may be.

First, I do think Baird is naive on certain points.   He says he isn't, but he is.   To believe that Baylor's religious identity is safe and secure given the current climate in higher education and given Baylor's ambitions to take its place among the elite research universities in this country is to be blind to the realities of hiring at the highest level of academic life. Even if Baylor were content to remain where it is in the intellectual pecking order of this country's universities, it would be difficult, given the prospective faculty hires coming out of contemporary graduate schools, to hold its own.

Second, for Baird to bring up Haywood Shuford in this argument is really tough for me. Baird has me on record as saying that Shuford "changed my life as surely and dramatically as if he had taken off the top of my skull and stirred my brains with a soup spoon." And I did mean that to be a compliment. Shuford was the most important intellectual influence on my life. Like Baird, I did not know, nor care, what religious views he held, nor whether he went to church or not. It is important to remember, however, why Shuford was so important to so many of us. It wasn't because he made fun of sappy and sentimental and half-baked religious ideas—which he certainly did. Ralph Lynn did all of that and we knew that he taught a Sunday School class. Ralph Wood does it today, or if he doesn't, he should. Shuford confronted most of us for the first time with incredibly high intellectual standards. And, let us be frank, the intellectual standards in many parts of Baylor at that time were shamefully low. He wouldn't let us get away with the intellectual laziness and sloppiness that were our meat and potatoes. He expected us to mean what we said—and to be able to explain what that was. He for the first time treated most of us as if we were adults intellectually. We must, however, not romanticize Shuford's influence on the entire student body. Most students dropped his courses during the first week. I had eight courses from him and none were larger than twelve or fifteen students—and most had under five students. I frequently had to help him recruit students so we would have enough students to make the course go.

That Shuford was more or less religiously orthodox had nothing to do with his power as a teacher. Of course, we need teachers like Shuford who show us what intellectual work of the most rigorous kind is like—but wouldn't it have been better if Shuford had been just as mean and demanding and impossible to satisfy and as frightening as he was, but also a Christian? Christians are supposed to be good, but they don't have to be nice. There is a danger around Christian groups that everybody goes soft and goody-goody. It is why Sunday School doesn't produce intellectuals. Out of some misunderstood sense of Christian charity we come to believe that we should be easy on students. This is nonsense, of course. Christian universities should be more rigorous, more demanding, more judgmental than secular universities since we believe that everything depends on our seeing the truth—and we should be constantly reminded that God is the truth.

What Shuford stood for was the uncompromising pursuit of the excellent in the life of the mind. We need people like that at Baylor, but those skills don't come branded with a religious label, nor with a non-religious one either.

Third, Baird says that Notre Dame's hiring is much more permissive than Baylor's and that Notre Dame nevertheless achieved academic excellence without oversight. If loose oversight is good enough for the Notre Dame goose, why not for the Baylor gander? A couple of points about that. As I have already said, I think that Notre Dame is in trouble at the hiring level, now that we have elevated standards so greatly. But Notre Dame was also first in this game, and we have picked off most of the high-powered Christian scholars already. There aren't many more to hire and we haven't left much for Baylor to pick up. I said before that we would have problems moving into the top ten philosophy departments without compromising our Christian character, but it is worse than that. It is not clear to me we can even hold our own. Our reputation depends on a small number of world-class figures, preeminently Al Plantinga and Alasdair MacIntyre, but also prominent figures like Ernan McMullin, Ralph McInerny, and David Burrell. The good news is that we have them all; the bad news is that they are all over seventy. And Al Plantinga is still climbing mountains. One slip on his part and we drop out of the top twenty in the philosophy gourmet report. The time may soon come when Notre Dame is sending people to Baylor to discover how you do it, rather than the other way around.

But I don't do justice to Baird's paper by picking away at these particular points. He is surely right that Baylor would be a better place, a better Christian university, were it more confidently to go about its business, were it not to talk so much about its being a Christian university. He says, "My dream is that of a Baylor so secure in its Christian heritage, so secure in its identity that it willingly embraces some faculty who are not full embodiments of that heritage." That's a pretty good dream. So why not embrace it?

I think we should embrace it as a matter of a long-run strategic goal. I hope that Don Schmeltekopf and Robert Sloan embrace it, too. It is the kind of Baylor University I would like to find on the banks of the Brazos a hundred years from now. Unfortunately, I feel that in order to build a university that embraces both the highest intellectual standards and the deepest Christian commitment, we now have to be more intentional in its design. That strategic goal demands tactics of hiring and faculty recruitment that now must inevitably seem pinched and crabbed to many of us. Let us all pray for the day when Bob Baird's vision cannot only define a strategic goal, but also less onerous tactics—a day when his vision can be realized. I don't think that day is here yet. We need Bob Baird's vision to remind us where we ultimately want to be. We need Don Schmeltekopf's tactical instincts to get us there.

V

Let me finally return for a personal word or two about Don. When the histories are written a hundred years from now about Christian higher education in our time (and we will have all gone to our Maker), we, of course, do not know what they will say. The efforts at Baylor to chart a bold new course for Christian higher education (and Don's role in that effort) might be just a blip, another good idea that was swamped by larger social trends. My colleague, Alasdair MacIntyre, our resident senior scholar at the ethics center I direct (and a professional and accomplished pessimist), is now banned from our planning meetings at the center because his response to virtually all of our planning initiatives is the same. He gives reasons in favor of the proposal under review and then continues almost always in the same words: "This is surely worthy of pursuit and we should go ahead with it, but, of course, we should recognize that all these efforts will almost certainly fail." This is so depressing not because we think he is wrong about the failure, but because we all suspect he may be right—but we wonder, why does he need to keep saying it? However, the future is uncertain and we should avoid cloud cuckoo-land optimists. There are formidable obstacles to Baylor's being successful in its current efforts. Given the trends in American higher education, many would say with MacIntyre, "It will almost certainly fail." And, of course, there are many both nearby and far away who will take pleasure in its failure. But it might not fail, and what a glorious thing that would be. Maybe these histories will write that a movement at a sleepy Texas university, associated with a table-thumping Baptist philosopher, grew into something that set higher education ablaze. In a hundred years, perhaps the world's scholars will flock to Waco, where the arts flourish, where great scholarly projects are commenced and completed, where a vibrant religious life is focused in a large, impressive and expensive (that for Ralph Wood) church at the center of the campus, where students thirst for knowledge and their thirst is slaked by a superb faculty, where, people say, there's been nothing like it since the University of Paris in the thirteenth century. And who cares that we still beat Texas only once every ten or fifteen years.

It is certainly the case that the vision articulated by Don Schmeltekopf and others at this university has shown the capacity to inspire others. It is not, alas, the high culture available at the Dr. Pepper Museum that has attracted some of the most talented young scholars in America to Baylor in recent years. There is a sense that something important is happening at Baylor. That is what lured Tom Hibbs and Rob Miner from Boston College and Steve Evans from Calvin, Bob Roberts from Wheaton, Ralph Wood from Wake Forest—and I could go on. I know this vision retains the power to dazzle and entice, and as the community of scholars committed to this vision grows on this campus, its attractiveness will only increase. At a time when teaching and research in large stretches of the humanities is moribund at many prestigious secular universities, the possibility of building a great Christian university, freed from the strictures of know-nothing fundamentalism and the insipid pieties of the politically correct but soulless modern university, is enormously exciting. We will just have to see what happens. I can't wait to see.

Don Schmeltekopf must get great credit for making this vision so dazzling and so seductive—and, above all, so possible to realize. Great ideas are a dime a dozen (especially around universities); the institutional structures and financial resources to realize those ideas are never easy to come by. Don has dedicated his career to the frequently thankless task of making an institutional structure capable of sustaining this ideal a reality. It has been a pleasure for me personally to be his friend over the last decade, and it has been an honor to follow him into battle in this great war of ideas being fought over the soul of the university. He has labored to good purpose in the vineyard of Christian higher education. He has weeded the rows, chopped away at the dead branches, and nurtured the green shoots. And we are all the better for his efforts.